Hope in the Wilderness

Spiritual Reflections for When God Feels Far Away

Hope in the Wilderness

Spiritual Reflections for When God Feels Far Away

Noel Forlini Burt

FOREWORD BY Jerry Sittser, author of
A Grace Disguised: How the Soul Grows Through Loss

CASCADE *Books* · Eugene, Oregon

HOPE IN THE WILDERNESS
Spiritual Reflections for When God Feels Far Away

Cascade Books
An Imprint of Wipf and Stock Publishers
199 W. 8th Ave., Suite 3
Eugene, OR 97401

www.wipfandstock.com

PAPERBACK ISBN: 978-1-5326-8934-5
HARDCOVER ISBN: 978-1-5326-8935-2
EBOOK ISBN: 978-1-5326-8936-9

Cataloguing-in-Publication data:

Names: Forlini Burt, Noel, author.

Title: Hope in the wilderness : spiritual reflections for when God feels far away / Noel Forlini Burt.

Description: Eugene, OR: Cascade Books, 2022 | Includes bibliographical references.

Identifiers: ISBN 978-1-5326-8934-5 (paperback) | ISBN 978-1-5326-8935-2 (hardcover) | ISBN 978-1-5326-8936-9 (ebook)

Subjects: LCSH: Christian life. | Bible—Criticism, interpretation, etc. | Biography—Noel Forlini Burt.

Classification: BS511.3 F665 2022 (print) | BS511 (ebook)

For the members of Academy #41, Camp Sumatanga, Gallant, Alabama,
who have taught me to pray in the wilderness.
And for Spike,
who has accompanied me there.

Contents

Foreword

St. Augustine set the standard, and none of us will ever reach it. Some works of literature and art are simply that good. Still, his *Confessions* does provide a model for how the rest of us can reflect on the story of our lives, whether such reflections make it to print or not. Augustine teaches us how important it is—how necessary, really—to think about our stories, not in a vacuum, as if the self had only the self to understand itself, but within the community of faith and in light of the redemptive plan of God.

I call Augustine's *Confessions* a "theological memoir." In the book there are two story lines unfolding at the same time. There is, on the one hand, his memory of events. Augustine's ransacking of the pear orchard comes to mind immediately as one such example. There is, on the other, God's purpose in those same events. Was it merely a boyhood prank, pure foolishness and immaturity? Or was it something other, a supposedly innocent act that was far more serious, destructive, and deadly than Augustine could have imagined? As Augustine learned, he loved the sin for the pure pleasure of committing the sin itself.

There is a reason why I begin with Augustine. He created the model of the theological memoir. Many others have used and developed it. Among them is Noel Forlini Burt. Her delightful and insightful *Hope in the Wilderness* is indeed a theological memoir. Like Augustine's *Confessions*, it tells the story of a journey. It begins at a camp in Alabama, which serves as a metaphor for security, belonging, and home. It leads to a campus in Texas—Baylor University—where Burt lands a post as a lecturer in biblical studies.

Much to her surprise, Baylor becomes a metaphor for wilderness. But Burt keeps returning to the camp, where she wrestles with God, gains insight, finds peace, and discovers her true calling.

Burt's story is anything but simple and sentimental. Into the narrative she weaves deep reflection, often using stories from the Old Testament as her guide and inspiration. Those stories help her make sense of her own difficult and perilous story. There is Elijah arriving at the Holy Mountain of God, where he enters into a terrifying and healing silence, the silence of God. There is Hagar abandoned and left alone in the wilderness, stripped of family, security, and identity, where she discovers she is not in fact alone. There is Esau trading his birthright for a bowl of soup.

Burt shows us how to read and tell our own stories in light of these biblical stories and ultimately the redemptive story. She speaks with honesty about her exile in Texas. She was left wondering how a cherished position, the envy of most academics because of the prestige of the position and reputation of the university, could have thrust her into such a barren and lonely wilderness. As she writes so eloquently, "I had a profound sense that I didn't belong anywhere." She was a "heart person working in a head position." "I've misplaced myself," she lamented, "unsure of where I am."

She had no map to follow either. "There is no orientation to wilderness. . . . It just happens to you, and you hope to God that God is somewhere nearby when it happens." Wendell Berry observed that we are called to live the "given life," not the "planned life." Burt had planned her life. But it didn't work out the way she had expected. The wilderness forced her to figure out how to live the "given life."

She never traveled completely blind because her eyes were wide open. She is uncommonly observant. Little escapes her. She set her mind and heart to learn what she could along the way. The wilderness exposed her quest for achievement and desire for control. But it also weaned her from those same attachments. The wilderness led her a long way from home. But she found a way to return home again, too. The wilderness became a profoundly lonely place. But in the end she discovered a sense of belonging and security.

Burt knows how to write. I found her prose a delight, insightful and deep but never turgid and unnecessarily complex. It is more akin to a moving river than a stagnant lake. She writes with the mind of an academic but also with the heart of a real human being who hasn't figured everything out yet. Her style has a nice pace to it, a kind of liturgical rhythm. In most chapters she repeats one line at just the right times. "God is the great silence." "In the struggle is the formation." "I want to be the name you give me." "Give me room to work." "Yell all you want. I'm not going anywhere." This liturgical sensibility draws the reader back to the central theme, like a mother's quiet whisper to a young child, "I love you."

Augustine's *Confessions* is out of reach. But Burt's *Hope in the Wilderness* is not. She shows us how to reflect honestly, biblically, and redemptively on our own stories. Her reflections invite readers to examine their own story and calls them to do so in light of the big story. I smiled a lot when reading it. I paused a lot. I thought a lot. Far from being sensational, as many stories are, Burt's story is profoundly human, ordinary, and accessible, which made the book all the more compelling to me. If Augustine's example inspires people like Noel Forlini Burt, then thank God for Augustine.

And thank God for Noel Forlini Burt, too.

GERALD L. SITTSER
Professor Emeritus, Whitworth University,
and author of, among other books, *A Grace Disguised*

Introduction

Sumatanga

IF YOU'RE WILLING TO strap on a good pair of hiking shoes and sweat your way over a mile straight uphill, the view of the cross overlooking the mountains at Camp Sumatanga will take your breath away. Aptly named "A Place of Rest and Vision," Sumatanga is a Methodist camp just north of Birmingham, Alabama. Though it does not boast exactly the vista described in Annie Dillard's *Pilgrim at Tinker Creek*, with its quintessentially Alabamian tree cover and rolling hills, I like to think that Sumatanga captures a bit of the holy. If you find yourself in a season where you're a little bit lost, or a little bit disoriented, Sumatanga is a good place to go.

It was during such a season, one in which I found myself profoundly *disoriented,* that I arrived at Sumatanga for orientation to what I've come affectionately to call "monk camp."

No, I'm not a monk.

I'm a thirty-nine-year-old married WASP with deep ties to the deep South and even deeper ties to the friends I've made there. In August of 2018, I began certification in spiritual formation through the Upper Room Academy for Spiritual Formation, returning to Sumatanga every three months for two years. Those two years as a member of Academy #41 are about as close to monkhood as I'm likely ever to get.

I've taken no vows in religious orders except, I suppose, for a vow to move my husband and our big orange cat halfway across the country, from our home of Birmingham, Alabama, to Waco,

Texas, home of the Fixer Uppers and . . . not much else. For the past six years, I guess you could say I've been a member of the order of "The Most Holy Fixer Uppers," the religion faculty at Baylor University. And no, I've never met Chip or Joanne, and I couldn't begin to tell you anything about interior design. Most of my furniture is homemade and falling apart, or purchased from Target when I was still in college. Most recently my husband and I kicked an old and broken recliner to the curb with a sign that read, "Rest in Pieces."

So, I am most decidedly not a monk, and I can't tell you anything about interior design, only that I wish that particular recliner a happy afterlife.

The things I *can* tell you about are relatively few. I can tell you where to get the best cappuccino you've ever had in your life (*O'Henry's Coffees. For the record, my favorite location is the one on 18th Street South, Homewood, Alabama*). I can tell you that if you're a runner, it's probably better to stretch first (*but I never do*). After nine years of graduate study and about an equal amount of time teaching, I can tell you a couple of things about the Bible (*although I'm not nearly as certain of as much as I used to be*).

And I can tell you about the wilderness. No, I'm not talking about actual wilderness. I'm talking about deep wilderness seasons of the soul. About the seasons when there's some kind of disorientation happening in your life, caused by any number of things: the loss of a dream, the crumbling of your sense of self, the prolonged waiting for that thing you're desperately hoping for, the deep sadness that *has a name (illness, family tragedy, loss of a job, the list goes on and on*), and the deep sadness that you don't even know *how to name*. All you know is that it's an invisible companion, one who is with you when you wake up in the morning and who is there with you when you turn off the light on your bedside table at night.

I can tell you about wilderness seasons of the soul, because it was during such a season that I arrived at Sumatanga for the first time. And on that first day of orientation, I heard the following words: *In the struggle is the formation.*

These were the first words that I heard—*really heard*—during my orientation to monk camp. For the next two years, I would hear those same words, a favorite saying of the academy, repeated often: *In the struggle is the formation.*

When you travel to the same place every three months for two years, you're just about guaranteed to see it in all kinds of weather, even in Alabama where the seasons aren't always very pronounced. Since that first visit in August of 2018, I've been to Sumatanga in every season and in all kinds of weather. I've been there when the Alabama heat was so oppressive that you couldn't walk two feet without sweating through your clothes. I've been there when a rare winter snow blanketed the trees, magically, until you slip and tumble down one of the rolling hills I usually love so much. And I've been there when half the week was like a monsoon, muddying the trail around the lake, and the other half of the week was dry, shrinking the muddy patches like a wound just beginning to heal. Depending on the season, Sumatanga always looked a little different, but the words I heard were always the same—*in the struggle is the formation.*

During my wilderness season living in Texas, that statement became a liturgy, sacred words that shaped my shared life with God. What I've discovered during these six years is that while there are many orientations we go through in our lives—orientation to school or to a job or to a new city, for example—there is no orientation to wilderness. It just happens to you, and you hope to God that God is somewhere nearby when it happens.

My season of wilderness, of disorientation, began when I was offered my dream job as a religion professor at Baylor. Landing that job was one of the great shocks of my life, one that felt like providence. So after just a few months of marriage, my husband and I packed up our minimal belongings and our big orange cat and headed to a place we'd never been before. At Baylor, I would teach four classes a semester, most of them with sixty students in each (*quite a load, any academic will tell you*), participate in academic conferences, mentoring of students, thesis advising, service to the university, service to the department, service to the church,

3

universal and local, and if I wanted to advance in the academic world, maintaining a robust scholarly research and publication agenda. Meanwhile, my husband would struggle with unemployment and underemployment for over two years. Our big orange cat, who had been with me since college, would die. My father would suffer a series of heart attacks. Significant relationships would fracture and die. I was diagnosed with a chronic illness that, for a time, severely hampered my ability to do anything other than go to work and come home. We would struggle to find a church home in Waco. We would miss the twenty-year friendships we had forged in Alabama. Our own relationship would struggle under the weight of everything else. And I would enter an intense four-year depression that turned on its head everything I thought I knew about myself, about the world, and about God.

Ultimately, my wilderness was a combination of all these things, some harder than others, some that I don't even have the courage to name here. But at the root of it all was a profound sense that I didn't belong anywhere. Part of that meant facing the reality that the so-called "dream job" I landed at Baylor was definitely *someone's* dream—it just wasn't mine. I had given over a decade to my education and training and sacrificed a whole lot along the way, only to discover that I was a heart person working in a head profession. I felt trapped and confused, unsure what path to take. All the familiar paths of chasing achievement through hard work and sheer determination (*I'm an Enneagram 3, I'm told*), which had served me so well all my life, suddenly no longer served me. Those paths were well-trodden and well-worn, but somehow, I couldn't rely on them anymore to get me on the right path, mostly because I didn't know the right path. And through it all, God kept silent. For the first time, I couldn't will my way out. I was lost in the wilderness.

And the trouble with that is, I have a comically bad sense of direction. With an equal mix of glee and pity, my husband likes to tell the story of how I once got lost leaving our apartment from the back entrance. And I'll readily admit that it was two years before I stopped using my GPS to drive to my best friend's house, and even then I could only find her house if I took the same road to get there. Because my sense of direction is so bad, I almost never get lost. I'm always in control of where I go, always sure how to get there because I've prepared well beforehand.

In this wilderness season, what I've discovered is that in spite of my best efforts to keep my life, I lost my life anyway. During these six years in Texas, I've begun to wander down an unknown trail, one wholly unfamiliar to me. Wandering down an unknown trail is something my buttoned-up self, desperate to keep the life that she had, wouldn't have done six years ago. I've misplaced myself, unsure of where I am. Of course, Christian tradition tells us that it's when we finally give up the life we're holding onto so tightly, finally loosen our chubby-fingered grip on it, then we will stumble onto the right trail. Into the right life. Into the life that is ours with God—into the life God is already dreaming for us to have. Along my own journey, it feels simultaneously like I have died, and also—in the words of the sage Parker Palmer—that I'm on the brink of everything. I suppose only God knows, since God is the keeper of my life, of your life, of all our lives.

I don't actually know if I'll stumble onto the right path after all. What I do know is two things—all of us, no matter who we are and how successful we are—if we are awake to our lives at all, will find ourselves on an unfamiliar path. We will find ourselves in wilderness. And the other thing I know is this—*in the struggle is the formation.*

I know this not just because I have experienced it myself—I know it because God's people in all times and in all places have experienced it, including the Israelites, those restless nomads who captured the heart of God and who capture my heart every time I turn the pages to their story.

For much of their story, the Israelites are in wilderness, whether wandering in actual wilderness following their release from slavery in Egypt on the way to the promised land; or in exile away from their home, an experience the prophets described as a wilderness. As a whole, biblical wilderness, as depicted in Exodus through Deuteronomy, or used as metaphor for exile in Isaiah and

5

Jeremiah, or even in the life of Jesus, involves many things, among them: disorientation, waiting, suffering, restlessness, confusion, spiritual malaise, stripping away of all the usual things upon which we rely, darkness, and, most surprisingly, *encounter with God*. And grace—lots of it. Grace upon grace, upon grace. Grace is learning, one way or another, that we are not what we do, or what we have, or what others think of us.[1] Life with God is a journey of allowing ourselves to be loved by God, and to trust that that is enough. And if it takes journeying with God into the wilderness to understand that, then so be it. All of this is grace, from the first syllable of God's invitation to the final moment when we come to die, buried by those who love us. All of it is grace.

And that's the thing about grace—it often comes to us when we're in the middle of nowhere. Grace comes as a surprise, the gift we never thought we'd get, in that place where we thought we'd never find God, or find much of anything at all. And there it is, right smack dab in the middle of the hardest place where we've found ourselves—that pearl of great price—life with God. Wilderness is part of our journey with God, and wilderness is grace, even if it's a place of deep disorientation. Even if it comes as a tap on the shoulder, inviting us to look in a different direction, and that direction just happens to be towards the wilderness. Grace is a voice inviting us to pay attention to our life. A voice inviting us to leave home, to discover that God is our true home.

What each of these biblical stories of wilderness appear to convey theologically is that wilderness is liminal space, space that is betwixt and between, space caught on the threshold from one thing to another. Space that is not intended for permanent habitation. Space that is not home. A space that teaches us to hold everything we think we know about God, about how the world works, about ourselves, loosely. Space that teaches us to hold loosely. And really, space that teaches us to let go.

Because the wilderness is the place in which God bids us to come and die. And to be reborn. And whatever is reborn in this space, in order for it to remain, it must remain in God.

1. Nouwen, *Home Tonight*, 38–39.

In the struggle is the formation.

None of this is natural. My natural inclination, for most of my life, has been to trust only myself. Trust myself to procure what I want, doggedly and aggressively to pull myself up by my own bootstraps (*okay, by my own flip flops*). This is certainly natural behavior, but it's not Christian behavior. It's rather the behavior of one who has not yet learned to die. In the wilderness, we can't make a pretense of relying on God while secretly living as functional atheists, really relying on ourselves. If we've truly been to the wilderness, we know that only God is able. The wilderness is the place where God bids us to come and die.

In the struggle is the formation.

I don't really have any answers. I know just two things, really. First, I know that in this current cultural moment, as we navigate together a global pandemic that has stretched longer than any of us probably imagined, deep political and racial unrest, and suffering in so many places, wilderness is a space we all inhabit right now, in one way or another. And second, I know my own story, and that is what I offer here as a companion for our wilderness journeys, both collective and individual. Not because I have any particular wisdom to share, but because, for me, writing is a form of prayer.

And so I offer my own, meager words as a prayer, along with this prayer from Thomas Merton, who was an *actual monk* (*instead of a pretender like me*):[2]

> My Lord God, I have no idea where I am going. I do not see the road ahead of me. I cannot know for certain where it will end. Nor do I really know myself, and the fact that I think I am following your will does not mean that I am actually doing so. But I believe that the desire to please you does in fact please you. And I hope I have that desire in all that I am doing. I hope that I will never do anything apart from that desire. And I know that if I do this you will lead me by the right road, though I may know nothing about it. Therefore will I trust you always though I may seem to be lost and in the shadow of death.

2. Merton, *Thoughts in Solitude*, 79.

I will not fear, for you are ever with me, and you will
never leave me to face my perils alone.

Merton's is a prayer out of the wilderness. While his words
are more eloquent than my own, they do capture something of the
spirit of this book. In these pages, you will watch me leave home
(*part of all our faith journeys*), eat more than one bowl of soup during cold winters when God didn't seem to have anything else on
the menu, yell at God a little (*okay, a lot*), smash a few of my idols
of choice, enter into the Great Silence in order to hear God (*part of
the Liturgy of the Hours in Christian tradition*), discover different
names for God and different names for myself, build a house like
the Israelites in exile, and, ultimately, find my way home to God.

Through it all, what I've discovered is those first words at my
orientation to monk camp are not only true—but are a liturgy for
the wilderness.

In the struggle is the formation.

I

Stalking Muskrats

I WAS PRETTY LITTLE when I started sneaking off to quiet places to read stories. On childhood vacations, I was the tiny visitor in the hotel lobby, a book on my lap beside a roaring fire. In college, I found a favorite park bench, the one underneath the trees overlooking the same divinity school I would attend years later. And at Camp Sumatanga, it was the fireplace in the lobby, still the coziest spot I can think of on a dark February morning before everyone else arrives for morning prayer. While each of these locations is special to me, it isn't so much the location that's important. It's the story that matters. Stories have power to transport us to other worlds, or to lean in closer to our own world, examining it with greater clarity and deeper empathy. Like a faithful friend who poses an evocative question at just the right time and in just the right way, stories help us to tell the truth about our lives. It was during a season of wilderness when I read just such a story, Annie Dillard's *Pilgrim at Tinker Creek*. In this Pulitzer Prize-winning book, among other things, Dillard devotes nearly twenty pages to her experience stalking a muskrat.

I'm happy to tell you that mine is not a story about stalking a muskrat (*especially since I don't even know what a muskrat looks like*). I've also never been to Tinker Creek, but I have been to Sumatanga, and it is there that I began to stalk my own life, much in the way Dillard stalked that wily old muskrat.

Our experiences of wilderness force us to do that—*pay attention*, I mean.

It is often through the experience of wilderness that God not only catches our attention—but our everything.

In my case, it didn't happen all in a moment. I wasn't Moses at the burning bush, wandering the wilderness one moment and suddenly sent off in a new direction in the next. Most of the time, the art of paying attention is slow work. Muskrats scamper out of view much faster than a soul opens to God. Nevertheless, through a series of experiences, many of them at Sumatanga, I began to ask whether the plans I had for my life were the same plans God had for my life.

I began to pay attention.

And when I began to pay attention, I realized that for much of my journey with God, I had taken a road marked "Achievement," rarely stopping long enough to assess whether that road was meaningful, or divinely ordained. The things I paid attention to were accumulating letters behind my name and awards on my wall. If I stalked anything, it wasn't a muskrat and it certainly wasn't my own life. I was much too busy for that, chasing upward mobility, status, and my own certainty that God had blessed the plans that I had created and called them "good," and even "very good." I had chased achievement with the same determination that I had chased a soccer ball down the field during my growing-up years, in a jersey emblazoned with the number one on it (*which I wore, I'm embarrassed to admit, without the slightest bit of irony*). I make this confession with a mixture of equal parts abnegation and acceptance. God is patient, and God will use anything in the world to get our attention and to draw us into the love that God has for us.

After all, God set an entire bush on fire just to get Moses to turn around, pay attention, and start chasing a life that actually mattered. Who knows how many bushes God set on fire that Moses didn't actually see? After all, you can stare at the same thing for a long time and never really see it. Maybe there were lots of bushes that blazed all around Moses, but it was this particular one that finally caught his attention. However it all happened, I always chuckle a bit when scholars pontificate about exactly what kind of bush it was that Moses saw. Some scholars think it was a blackberry bush, and I like that because it brings back fond memories of picking blackberries with two cute grannies in East Tennessee. I also like this interpretation because it reminds me that this was just an ordinary bush. And if this was just an ordinary bush, doesn't that mean that God can use the ordinary events of our lives to get us to pay attention?

Who knows if the scholars are right? I don't think it really matters. The poet Elizabeth Barrett Browning put it better, anyway: "Earth's crammed with heaven, And every common bush afire with God, But only he who sees takes off his shoes; The rest sit round and pluck blackberries."[1] In their own mystical way, the poets are often the ones that make the profoundest discoveries, while scholars like me sit around with blackberries in our teeth.

I don't know how any of it works, really. I just wonder if the ordinary moments, the impressions that we have about this or that, the feelings of restlessness or joy—I just wonder if these things are invitations to . . . *wonder*—feelings of surprise caused by the beautiful, the unexpected, the unfamiliar. And I wonder if these invitations to wonder are more frequent than we think and in fact, are all around us. Maybe there are far more ordinary blackberry bushes set ablaze by the wonder and the beauty and the joy and the surprise of God than we dare imagine.

That burst of joy you feel for no explicable reason, right there in the middle of an ordinary work meeting—what if that's God? What if that's God's invitation to enter into his love for you? That months-long restlessness you feel—what if that's God's invitation to look at your life and to move in a different direction? That surprising word of wisdom from a friend outside an ordinary movie theater on an ordinary Saturday night? Well, that's a word of wisdom that might just land you in seminary six months later (*I know, because it happened to me*). That pensive word from a coworker that's about her life—"Sometimes you have to leave home

1. Barrett Browning, *Aurora Leigh*, 234.

to discover that God is your true home"—but that pricks you to the heart—and you just know it's a message for you (*for the record, that one happened to me too, and that's exactly how I wound up in New Jersey, and now, in Texas*). That longing you have, the one that seems impossible until out of nowhere, you're stopped at a traffic light and suddenly you think, "What if it's possible after all?" What if that's God whispering a word of assurance? What if all the things we think are so ordinary, God has hallowed as extraordinary after all? What if all these ordinary things are actually God's invitations?

Someone once said that God can do immeasurably more than we can ask or imagine. Maybe that someone was right. It was just an ordinary blackberry bush, after all, and God set it on fire, kept it from being consumed, and invited Moses into life with himself.

Like I said, I don't really know how any of it works. I just know that as I began to pick a few blackberry seeds out of my teeth, the first thing I noticed was a Voice inviting me to a different kind of life than the one that I had been living. Like Moses and like so many of us, that Voice began to surface when I was living my ordinary life. Part of the rhythm of that ordinary life involved traveling back and forth between Texas and Sumatanga every three months. It was somewhere in the midst of that season when I began to notice and to name the voices I received as a child, voices that said: "Make a name for yourself. Achieve something. Become somebody important. Chase success."

At Sumatanga, I began to hear another Voice, one that invited me not to chase, but to belong. Deeply, wholly, to God. To myself. And to keep returning to those whose voices beckoned me to a more meaningful way of living in the world. As a result, I began to look in a whole new direction. Instead of looking up, I began to look down. I became convinced that to stalk my life, I had to go down into the deep caverns of my soul, where my true life with God in Christ is hidden. I began to pay attention to my life, to the Voice that was inviting me to look in a new direction.

Well, I told you mine wasn't a story about a muskrat, and that's true, it's not. Even so, Dillard's muskrat-stalking skills can offer us some collective wisdom. She describes her experience at

Tinker Creek, that beautiful patch of wilderness in Virginia, in this way: "Stalking the other way, I forge my own passage seeking the creature. I wander the banks; what I find, I follow, doggedly, like Eskimos haunting the caribou herds. I am Wilson squinting after the traces of electrons in a cloud chamber; I am Jacob at Peniel wrestling with an angel."[2] This is a kind of seeking that, Dillard claims, is something more akin to *stalking*.

Christians throughout the ages have stalked God—and their own lives—in a similar way. Those whose faith has been formed in this tradition call it the *Via positiva*, or the *cataphatic Way*. Many faithful Christians have traveled this path, comforted by the assurance that God can be pictured in ways both familiar and concrete. This is certainly scriptural. Jesus describes himself, after all, using concrete images. Jesus is the Vine. Jesus is the Light of the World. Jesus is the Good Shepherd. Jesus is the Way, the Truth, and the Life. I had, for much of my life, found comfort in these words. I could know who God was, and, so it seemed, I could know who I was, too.

And while there is nothing necessarily wrong with that old road, all of a sudden, I found the soles of my feet—and my soul—on a different path altogether.

Too many unplanned things had taken place for me to continue on the same road. For one thing, I was an achiever who suddenly felt too tired to achieve. My heart just wasn't in it anymore. I had spent nine years teaching and studying the Bible, only to discover that teaching the Bible in an academic way wasn't my calling. I was an Alabama native who thought I'd always live there with my husband and our big orange cat, until we didn't. One morning I woke up in my house in Texas, a big slobbering dog in my lap, wondering how any of it had happened. All the things I thought I knew about myself, declarative statements I had punctuated with exclamation points, began to curve into the curious shape of question marks. All the things that had felt certain, the things I had planned for myself, the things I felt so sure God was saying to me,

2. Dillard, *Pilgrim at Tinker Creek*, 186–87.

seemed like the subject of someone else's story. I was unsure if any of the roads I had taken were the right roads.

It was at Sumatanga that I rediscovered the writings of Thomas Merton, a twentieth-century Trappist monk I first encountered when I was in seminary. As so often happens to young seminarians, I was introduced to him before I had lived long enough to understand his ideas. At the time, his life seemed so strange, and so foreign to my own. I had no idea what it meant to be a monk, someone whose whole life was dedicated to God. Even now, I remain somewhat comically the type of Christian who affirms the poetic words of Flannery O'Connor: "The Christian faith is not a big electric blanket—it's the cross"—but packs a big electric blanket to take with me to monk camp anyway because, well, it's just so cozy (*did I mention that I'm not a real monk?*).[3] So for a long time, Merton's books collected dust on my shelf, his words inscrutable because I had not yet lived them.

Many years later, Merton is one of many great spiritual writers—some ancient, some modern—whose words have begun to find their way into the pages of my own story. In particular, a portion of Merton's prayer from *Thoughts in Solitude* captures the spirit of the wilderness I have felt during these six years in Texas: "My Lord God, I have no idea where I am going. I do not see the road ahead of me. I cannot know for certain where it will end. Nor do I really know myself."[4]

As Merton's words began to find a home in my lived experience, I realized the familiar *Via positiva* was a way that had closed. Maybe temporarily, maybe forever. It didn't matter—I just knew I needed to find another way. Well, if Dillard is to be believed, there's more than one way to stalk a muskrat. And if Christian tradition is to be believed, there's more than one way to stalk God, or your own life, too. Dillard acknowledges as much when she describes stalking a muskrat in yet a different way: "When I stalk this way, I take my stand on a bridge and wait, emptied. I put myself in the way of the creature's passage, like spring Eskimos at a seal's breathing

3. O'Connor, *Habit of Being*, 354.
4. Merton, *Thoughts in Solitude*, 79.

hole. Something might come; something might go."[5] This kind of seeking involves putting yourself in the path of the sought (*whether muskrat, God, or your own life*) and waiting, stilled, expecting that, perhaps, "something might come; something might go." This form of stalking doesn't feel like stalking at all, because here, we are human *beings* rather than human *doings*. There's nothing in particular that we *do*, except to wait quietly, emptying the self and its desires and waiting for the *sought* to come out of its hiding place. In stalking this way, Dillard says, "I found out the hard way that waiting is better than pursuing; now I usually sit on a narrow pedestrian bridge at a spot where the creek is shallow and wide. I sit alone and alert, but stilled in a special way, waiting and watching for a change . . ."[6] And as we wait, what may appear to us is not the thing we always assumed would appear; what may appear may not in fact be the thing we think we are waiting for, but something else altogether.

The fruit of this waiting may come as a disruption of our plans—where we are led, in a roundabout way, to something we never envisioned for ourselves but that more concretely expresses who God is and what God wants for us.

Admittedly, this particular way was not comfortable, and it did not come easily for me. There came a point, however, when my depression became so intense that *nothing* was all I *could* do. The experience was a roundabout way of my becoming a human *being* rather than a human *doing*, maybe for the first time in my life. As I continued to pay attention to this new, unknown way, I discovered that there are lots of names for this other way.

Hebrew tradition refers to it as the "roundabout way" of the wilderness. The writer of Exodus puts it this way: "When Pharaoh let the people go, God did not lead them by way of the land of the Philistines, *although that was nearer*; for God thought, 'If the people face war, they may change their minds and return to Egypt.' *So God led the people by the roundabout way of the wilderness* toward the Red Sea" (Exod 13:17–18 NRSV). They would one day make it

5. Dillard, *Pilgrim at Tinker Creek*, 186.
6. Dillard, *Pilgrim at Tinker Creek*, 189.

to the promised land—but they would have to travel through the wilderness first.

The roundabout way of the wilderness is a way that raises all kinds of questions: what road *is this* that I'm on? If I can't see the way, how will I know when I get there? Is there a . . . *there* . . . that I'm even traveling to? Who is the One—the uppercase One, always faithful and true, who invites us to take this path? We can think we know the sound of his voice, until suddenly, we're not so sure.

And who is the one—the lowercase one, doing her best to be faithful and true—but who fails every time the path curves in a direction she did not expect? She is the one whose every freckle we know so well that we scarcely need a mirror to point them all out—until one day, all of a sudden we see her through a mirror darkly, too.

If it feels like, in every way, the way has closed, that's probably because it has.

The Quakers have a name for this disorienting experience, too: *way closing*, painful places of transition where one life has ended and an uncertain future is dimly lit around a darkened corner. *Way closing* might be a blessing, or it might involve tragedy. Change of any kind, good and bad, can still disorient us. A major move, falling in love, the birth of a child, the loss of a job, the dissolution of a marriage, a cancer diagnosis, the questions naturally raised by entering middle age, or the door slammed in the face of a lifelong dream—each of these are *ways* that close—taps on the shoulder, invitations to look in different directions, to take the unexpected, even the roundabout way. *Way closing* reminds us that God is the only One who can make a way when there seems to be no way. God alone can forge a path in the wilderness.

Among Christians in the medieval period, that other "way" was the negative way, called the *Via negativa*, or the *apophatic Way*. Practiced by many earnest seekers, including the Christian mystics, those wonderfully weird and wise men and women of the High Middle Ages, the *Via negativa* is dark, still, and quiet. Instead of looking for God in the same images that have always given you comfort, you begin to strip those images away. Instead, you take a path of negation, acknowledging that in all the important things—God and your life with God—certainty gives way to mystery and to unknowing. All you do is put yourself . . . *somewhere* . . . and empty yourself of your expectations that what appears look a particular way. Stilled, silent, emptied, you wait and watch for whatever is sought (or, to use Dillard's word, *stalked*) to emerge from that darkness.

For Dillard, this way, like the *Via positiva*, also involves a muskrat or two.

However it happens to us and however we choose to respond, if nothing else, the roundabout way of the wilderness is an invitation to do what saints and scholars across the ages have advised—*listen to your life, because that is where God has disguised himself*—in the nooks and crannies and crevices of your life in all its particularity, in all its pain and joy, uncertainties and doubts, boredom and exhilaration, God has disguised himself there. And when "Way" has closed, there you find him—God in disguise.

The roundabout way of the wilderness is the way we could have never planned, and it's often the way we'd never choose to take, if given the choice. It's the God-in-disguise way, and it disrupts our plans. But as Parker Palmer has said, when "Way" closes, the rest of the world opens up.[7] Which is to say that God—who comes disguised as your life—begins to open up when all the other unnecessary things get stripped away—and you begin to relinquish the best-laid plans you had for your life. The roundabout way of the wilderness is the God-in-disguise way, an invitation to see if the life you are living is the life God has planned for you.

All of this means, of course, that you have to pay attention. You have to listen to your life, because that is how God speaks.

If all else fails, and you're not sure how to go about it, stalk your life the way Dillard describes stalking that wily old muskrat. Something may come of it, or nothing may come of it, but at least it'll give you some practice in the art of paying attention.

7. Palmer, *Let Your Life Speak*, 54.

2

Bowls of Soup

SOMEWHERE TOWARD THE END of the first year of my wilderness in Texas, I began to wonder if I had misheard the Voice telling me to leave home.

The bank account was overdrawn, bills were overdue, relationships had fractured, and I felt overworked and alone. Nothing had turned out like I had thought. Fearing my situation might never change, some days I was torn between home and the dream of collegiate teaching. But most days, I was just desperate to go home.

And so when, for a brief moment, it felt like Way had opened, I decided to take matters into my own hands. An opportunity presented itself to go home, and it felt simultaneously like a sure thing, and also like my salvation. At least, until I heard these words from a trusted mentor: *"My dear, if you make this decision, you will be trading your birthright for a bowl of soup."*

It was one of the most haunting things anyone has ever said to me: *You will be trading your birthright for a bowl of soup.*

Immediately, those words reminded me of the familiar story of the patriarch Jacob in the wilderness. It had been the subject of my doctoral dissertation, and it's a story I've come to know like the back of my hand.

The first time we encounter the twins Jacob and Esau as adults, the wily Jacob is bent over, cooking a pot of seasonal soup. Esau has just spent the day hunting and he comes home, famished and exhausted. In typical brotherly behavior, Jacob says something like this: *"If you give me what I want, I'll give you what you want."* Jacob goes on to say that what he wants is Esau's inheritance, what the Israelites called a birthright. And just like that, we find ourselves circling around God's promises, because a birthright is a promise. A birthright is a divine intent, whispered over a life before that life has ever come to be.

It is a Voice that whispers, *"Your birthright is who you are. Here are your gifts. Handle them with care and don't bury them in the ground, because they are yours. Your birthright is My 'Yes' over your life. You don't have to grab at it, barter for it, or worry that it belongs to someone else. It's a gift—just receive it."*

A birthright is like grace. We can't earn it, because it's already ours. All we do is bend our ear to the ground and listen for it. *Our birthright is who we are.*

Theologian and social activist Howard Thurman would call it the sound of the genuine: *"There is something in every one of you that waits and listens for the sound of the genuine in yourself. It is the only true guide you will ever have. And if you cannot hear it, you will all of your life spend your days on the ends of strings that somebody else pulls."*[1]

And there Esau was, at the other end of the string that Jacob pulled, trading his birthright for a bowl of soup. Is it possible to give our birthright away and never get it back? Once it's done, can it be undone? In that moment, Esau didn't care. "What use is it to me?" Esau asked (Gen 25:32). "I just need to eat." Through gritted teeth, Esau, we're told, "spurned his birthright" (Gen 25:34).

It was a place in which I also found myself. And admittedly, it was a frightening place to be—angry, afraid, and too tired to care if I had thrown away God's promise to me. Is it possible to give a birthright away and never get it back? Once it's done, can it be undone? I wasn't sure, but at the time, like Esau, I didn't care. *"What use is it to me?"* I asked God in that wilderness season of my life. *"I just need to go home."*

---

1. Thurman, "Sound of the Genuine."

And there it was—a bowl of soup on the table, what looked like a sure thing. I did my best to grab it, apologized to my dear mentor, telling him I had made my decision, and phoned home to my husband to start purchasing moving boxes. And in one of the more shocking plot twists of my own story, God took the bowl of soup off the table. God stepped in, and God said *no*. It shattered me. For a long time, I remained locked in the anger and sadness stages of grief. I remember that it was summer outside, but inside of myself, I struggled to stay warm to God and to my own life. A winter of grief set in.

And then winter actually came, and I found myself returning home to Alabama, this time not to visit friends or to escape the wilderness—but to embark on a two-year journey of certification in spiritual formation. On a cold February morning at Sumatanga, I poured out whatever was left of my cold heart to my spiritual director. She listened quietly for a long time, until finally, she broke the silence: *"Noel, do you believe that God desires your good?"* Immediately, I wanted to deflect, to list everything on my spiritual resume. Lifelong churchgoer. Lay leader. Seminary trained. Religious professional.

"Of course I do."

A trained spiritual director, she saw right through it. And so, I suspect, did God.

"Do you believe God that God desires your good?"

It was a question that cut to the core of my own wilderness experience, inviting a real response. I sat down to think about it at what has become for me a holy place, the fireplace in the lobby of Camp Sumatanga. As I was pondering this question, my friend Kathy smiled at me and asked the Sumatanga staff, *"Do you mind turning on the fireplace for her? Noel loves this spot so much."* Here I was, thinking that maybe God needed to purify me of my selfishness—that perhaps dangling an opportunity to go home and taking it away might finally cure me of my unredeemable selfishness. Maybe that's how God works. Maybe God would dangle a good gift in front of me, only to take it away so that my selfishness could be redeemed. Perhaps then my price will have been paid. Then for the first time during that cold February week at Sumatanga, the fireplace came on. For the first time in a long time, that small act of grace warmed my heart, reminding me that God is good.

"What if that's not how God works?" I wondered. What if God is not a cruel parent who says my selfishness must be atoned for through self-flagellation? What if God has already atoned for my selfishness on the cross? What if Kathy's turning on the fireplace for me is an example of a person who will not give stone when a child asks for bread (Matt 7:11)? What if God wants to give not just appropriately—but even abundantly—to his children? *Even to this child?* Even to me, in all my selfishness and sin? What if God doesn't punish cruelly? What if God *wants* to bless me? What if God *does* want to give me the blessing that is rightfully mine—not to barter for it or manipulate someone else out of it—but just to ask for it, like a child?

"We are closest to grace in those places where we feel most like a child." In that moment in front of the fireplace, I was transported back to my pastor's office many years ago, where I had listened tearfully as he had spoken those words. The trouble is, I had never really been a child, arms open, yielded and still on God's lap.

It's one of the hardest words I've ever had to hear from my pastor: *"Noel, I actually think you're a lot like Jacob. You've found out how to make your way in the world, just like he did."*

For most of my life, I had been more like the patriarch Jacob, the one hunched over a bowl of soup, eager to trade soup for the birthright of someone else. Eager to *be* anyone other than myself. Fully capable, it seems, of working as though everything depends on me. Less able, it seems, to pray as though everything actually depends on God.[2] The truth of the matter is this—after all this time with God, I didn't understand grace at all.

"Boy, that's some soup that sure is hard to swallow," I told him.

"I know," he grinned. *"But it's probably better to be Jacob than to be Esau."*

Poor old Esau, the one Scripture hardly remembers. And Jacob, the one who would go on to wrestle with God and live to tell

2. As taught by Ignatius of Loyola (after Augustine).

about it. The one who would take his place in a long line of people who walked with God. Jacob, the one who's quick to learn how to achieve success in the world but slow to understand grace. Jacob, the one who's skilled in making soup but not so sure that God loved him for who he was. Jacob, the one who tricks his own father into giving him Esau's blessing. Jacob, the one who even says: "I am Esau," to an aging, vulnerable father with bleary eyes and an open heart (Gen 27:19). Jacob, the one who's eager to earn everything that he has, through any means possible, but whose love for God is conditional: "Then Jacob made a vow, saying, '*If* God will be with me, and will keep me in this way that I go, and will give me bread to eat and clothing to wear, so that I come again to my father's house in peace, *then* the Lord shall be my God . . .'" (Gen 28:20–21 NRSV). Jacob, the one who, even in the wilderness, was still trying to bargain with God about how to live his life. The one who didn't seem to have the foggiest idea about how life with God actually works. I was like that guy. It was hard soup to swallow.

It's taken me a long time to accept this about myself, but here it is: I wanted to live my life on my own terms. I was always scheming to ensure not so much that God was my Savior, but my patron. God already knew that about me, but it took entering into the wilderness to discover it for myself. It took entering into the wilderness, that most surprising of places, for Jacob to encounter God too: "'Know that I am with you and will keep you wherever you go, and will bring you back to this land; for I will not leave you until I have done what I have promised you.' Then Jacob woke from his sleep and said, 'Surely the Lord is in this place—and I did not know it!'" (Gen 28:15–16 NRSV) Jacob encounters God, not when he is safely in his homeland, but when he is in the wilderness, on the run, disoriented about himself and about his life. It is in the wilderness that Jacob begins a journey with God that changes him. For Jacob, ultimately that change would happen in darkness, wilderness's closest companion.

Theologian Frederick Buechner would call it a "magnificent defeat," and indeed it was.[3] Fearful of facing up to his crooked

3. Buechner, "Magnificent Defeat."

past, Jacob stops somewhere in the middle of nowhere and offers the first night prayer in the Bible. In a prayer reminding God of his promise to protect him along the long journey home, Jacob humbles himself before the One who had been with him all along: "I am not worthy of all the steadfast love and all the faithfulness that You have shown your servant" (Gen 32:10a NRSV). And Jacob spends the night at a place called Peniel, which means "Face of God." Here, Jacob would be forced to face not just God—but his whole life. Or, as *The Book of Common Prayer* puts it, all that he had done and all that he had left undone.

And sometime after God gives him a limp that he will never lose, God asks him a curious thing: "What is your name?" (Gen 32:27). And of course, God, this One who is Himself beyond all names (Phil 2:9–11), already knows Jacob's name. Indeed, he knows Jacob's whole life: all Jacob's deception and self-deception, all his unspoken fear and shame, all the people he's loved and all the people whose love he's been desperate for, all his dreams for the future. God looks into Jacob's face and asks Jacob to face it all too: "I am Jacob," he finally admits (Gen 32:27). And I imagine that the rest of Jacob's speech went something like this: *"I am the crooked one, the cheat, the bargainer, the one who grabs people by the heel so I can take what they have. I am Jacob. That is my name, that is who I have been."*

"Good," I imagine God whispered. *"Now I can finally bless you."*

So somewhere in the middle of that dark, wilderness space, God defeats Jacob, and he gives him a new name, Israel, the one who has wrestled with God. It took Jacob journeying to the middle of nowhere to own up to who he was. It took Jacob journeying into the wilderness to understand that grace, God's deepest blessing, is never a *thing* to be earned or bargained for. And I'd bet my life on it—every time it got damp or the weather changed and Jacob's bones ached—he remembered that night. Grace—we never forget where we were when we first received it. We never forget where we were when God begins to change us.

"Spiritual maturity is accepting ourselves and our origins as nonnegotiable," my pastor told me one day. It may be hard soup to swallow sometimes, but our story is itself a gift. Every bit of it is grace, from our first cry as a newborn, to our cries in the wilderness, and to the cry of our very last breath. All of it is grace, this thickly textured story of our lives. Wilderness does that—disorients us just enough so that we actually open ourselves to God.

It would be during the third year of my wilderness season in Texas where I would cry—and change—the most. As I slumped down in my favorite chair that February in front of the fireplace at Camp Sumatanga, I prayed the most honest prayer I have ever prayed: *"I came to You long ago, like Jacob, demanding a blessing. I was strong enough to wrestle with you then, but I'm in a different place now. I can't wrestle with you, I can't demand anything from you. I would beg and plead, but I'm too tired for that. I am very vulnerable right now. I need you—you have me. I have been defeated. My pride is gone, and Noel is gone. All I have is you. I have no power, no strength left. I am shattered, glass shards on a floor. Perhaps now you can finally, really, use me."*

When Jacob wrestled God, God left him with a limp so that if he forgot the encounter, his body never would. And in that moment alone with God in front of the fireplace, I recalled a picture of my husband and me just before we got married and moved to Texas. The change in us both was striking. Our faces are different now. Our bodies are different now. They are weaker, heavier, weighty and weighted down. I remembered that picture of us both, young, smiling, happy. I realized that all that I had held onto, all that I had counted as something that I could count on, was gone.

And so I prayed: *"I do not even have myself. That self has been crushed. I can fight no more. I can work no more. I can work no harder. I need grace. I cannot save myself from this season. Noel has been defeated—you may have me. I want the name you give to me. And I want to trust, no more to be afraid, but to trust in a Person other than myself. I am too weak, too sinful. You alone are not weak. You alone are not sinful. You alone have the power to remake me. Remake me into whatever and whomever you want. Help me to live from a center of belovedness, to navigate this wilderness holding your hand like a child. To hold your hand. To be yours. You alone are good. You alone have the power to save. To heal. To make the sin sick whole. To free. To redeem. To call by name. I have been running from, raging against. Now I run to. Now I let myself be held. Now I become myself. Now I become. Now. Now I am born again. Now. I do not know who this new person will be, but I do know to whom she will belong."*

While I am a bit removed now from that prayer, I remain in that same wilderness season. The only difference now is that I am less apt to trade my birthright for a bowl of soup, and more willing to bend my ear to the ground, listening to the sound of the truly genuine—the sound of grace. In listening to the sound of the genuine, I am listening for my true self, with all its birthright gifts and blessings God whispered over me before I was born. And what I hear, when I incline my ear to the ground, is the whisper of God's love for all people, even me.

3

Yelling at God

On a clear morning, the trees in Alabama appear to climb all the way up to the sky, curve around the rolling hills, and hug you on every side. I love Alabama for many reasons, and its abundance of trees is at the top of my list. When I finally agreed to buy a house in Texas, the trees in our backyard were a key selling feature because they reminded me of home. In the fall and winter, I often sit on our back deck, roasting s'mores around our fire pit. Those mornings are peaceful, sweet chocolate on the end of a skewer, the big orange cat and the big slobbering dog by my side, watching the birds light on our deck and fly away again. There are other mornings, however, when the scene is decidedly less peaceful. Instead of roasting s'mores, sometimes I've gone out there to roast God. Which of the two happens more often? Well, let's just say that I haven't yet emptied my pantry of all the chocolate bars, and one particular autumn, my voice got hoarse from all the yelling.

I remember that it was a particularly beautiful, crisp November morning when I went out on my back deck to really let God have it.

"You've brought us out to this wilderness to let us die!"

I don't know how much of that God actually heard, but I do know that the dog's ears perked up.

You say a lot of things you don't mean in the wilderness.

"God, why on earth did I ever listen to you?"

"I'd rather go home and live in a cardboard box than this god-awful place." "I'm so done with you, God."

At the time, of course you mean every word that you yell in what you think is God's general direction. But God knows, all the yelling is just a symptom of the hurt that happens in the wilderness. I'm convinced that anger and sadness are really two sides of the same coin, and whether we're sad or mad just depends on what day of the week it happens to be.

We can think we're mad enough or sad enough to be totally done with God, but God gets the final say in these kinds of things. And the truth of the matter is that with God, it's never really over. We serve a God who dwells in eternity, a God without beginning and without end, a God who has loved us before we were born and who will go on loving us after we die. God is a circle whose center is everywhere and whose circumference is nowhere; there is no edge to God.[1]

"Yell all you want," God says, with a chuckle. "But I'm not going anywhere."

When the Israelites are hungry, scared, and beg Moses to go back to Egypt, Moses has a similar reaction. He's had it, and he goes out on his back deck to really let God have it.

"I can't do this by myself—it's too much, all these people. If this is how You intend to treat me, do me a favor and kill me. I've seen enough; I've had enough. Let me out of here" (Num 11:15 The Message).

It was God's mercy that I rediscovered the story of Moses and the Israelites in the wilderness when I did. While yelling at God might get bad press in some Christian circles, God's people have a history of hurling insults in his direction. For me, Moses's story was a clear depiction of a person of faith who wasn't afraid to have it out with God. Moses, the man the Bible lauds as more humble than anyone else on the face of the earth (Num 12:3); the man who, in his narrative eulogy is praised for the unequal wonders and signs he performed and for his intimacy with God (Deut 34:10–12); Moses spends a lot of time yelling at God in the

1. Mills, Upper Room Academy for Spiritual Formation Lecture.

wilderness. Among many other things, what I glean from Moses's relationship with God is this: yelling at God does not make me a "bad Christian." First of all, who knows what a "good Christian" is, anyway? I'm certain I've never met one. It's the people who think they're "good Christians" that we probably ought to watch out for, not the ones who worry that their anger is going to offend God. Here, a lot of us could stand to borrow a page or two from the prayer book of our Jewish sisters and brothers. Jewish tradition is steeped in this kind of prayer.

Jews call it *Hitbodedut*, a conversational prayer where you tell God how you feel, unedited. Moses's prayer in the wilderness is a form of this. He's angry because wilderness is hard and the Israelites complain constantly. Honestly, I can't say I blame them, but that's a different matter altogether. Moses must have realized that all his education in Egypt didn't prepare him for this ministry assignment. I've discovered something similar, and it's this: seminary training can't prepare you for the wilderness—only prayer can do that. And for prayer to be prayer, it must be honest. When we pray, we need to show up for prayer as our real selves, wearing our mismatched socks, the coffee stains on our shirt, and our just-tumbled-out-of-bed hair. And we need to be honest about what we feel: *"God, I'm mad at you, and I'm just not interested in talking to you today."*

"Yell all you want," God says with a chuckle. *"But I'm not going anywhere."*

"And guess what?" he adds, just for fun. *"You just prayed."*

A simple, honest sentiment like, *"God, I'm mad at you,"* is still prayer. In fact, I'm convinced it's this kind of prayer that's more likely to capture God's attention than my guilt-induced empty praise. While some churches might require our Sunday best, God will take us however he can have us, still in our pajamas, our mismatched socks, and our just-tumbled-out-of-bed hair. When we show up to pray, the only thing God requires is honesty.

It's a funny thing—sometimes we're praying and we don't even know it.

It was a morning like any other, nothing particularly significant about it, when I caught myself accidentally in prayer. With my coffee in hand and my just-tumbled-out-of-bed hair, I sat on the sofa to plan the day.

White beans and sausage in the Crock-Pot, that'll be a good side dish for the leftover pot roast. I'll have to go to the store later for the sausage.

A run at 4:30. If I wear my running clothes all day, that'll save me a step.

I probably have three hours to write before the dog wakes up and wants to play.

I'll return emails to my students after lunch.

Strangely, it was a casual question from my husband in the middle of my meal planning that did it. *"Hey, did you find out if you'll be teaching a summer class?"* And there it was, out of nowhere—one of those *Hitbodedut*, yelling kinds of prayers, the kind that send husbands scampering off to work. I don't know a person in the world who gets emotional while thinking about white beans and sausage, but somehow I did. A reservoir of emotion came spilling out, and if I wasn't so upset, I would have found it hilarious. I was angry in one moment and tearful in the next, and I told God (*and my poor husband*) exactly how I felt—*stuck*.

"You're angry because you've realized you've been climbing the wrong ladder and now you're stuck on it," my husband said, before leaving for work to let God and I sort it out together. I did feel stuck, stuck inside the choices I had made that had sent us far from home, stuck inside the hamster wheel of achievement and academic expectation, overworked and undernourished by the fast-food approach to teaching promoted by the academy, the only sure thing the signing of yet another contract obligating us to yet another year in the wilderness.

It wasn't just the place that felt far from home—it was the vocation itself. I had spent the better part of my adult life powered by coffee and certainty, the certainty that God had called me to teach. Eight years in, I knew I loved my students, but I also knew my students were the only part of it I still loved. Somehow, I had found myself simultaneously at a crossroads and at an impasse. That's the best way I can describe wilderness—it's a crossroads place where you decide what really matters to you. And it's also a stuck place, a place you can't seem to get out of, with its irredeemably monotonous terrain. How could the wilderness, with its barrenness, have cleared away just enough underbrush for you to see the truth about your life, only to trap you there? I felt like I carried everything on my shoulders, and I felt angry at God, at myself, at my husband, and at the individual and collective choices we had made. Here we were, stuck in the wilderness.

And so for the first time, I could understand Moses's anger. Although they could have taken a shortcut, early on God decides that wilderness will be part of the Israelites' journey. Fearing they will face war and be tempted to turn back, God leads them by the "roundabout way of the wilderness" instead (Exod 13:17–18). It doesn't appear that Moses has any say in the matter, nor does it appear that God explains his reasoning. Instead, they appear to travel in relative silence, one foot in front of the other, a pillar of cloud by day and a pillar of fire by night to guide their way.

For the last six years, that's all I've been able to do, too—just put one foot in front of the other. What I've discovered is that the wilderness will always be the "roundabout way." It's a roundabout way that befuddles us, that makes us fighting mad, that exhausts every last resource that we have. Yet in its own roundabout way, the wilderness also teaches us to pray. I went to Texas thinking I would learn how to teach. As it turns out, God took me this roundabout way to *teach me* about many things, chiefly prayer.

One thing I've learned about prayer is that I need to be honest with God and myself about my anger. Otherwise, we're just wasting each other's time. Those of us who grew up in churches or in homes where it wasn't safe or okay to express our feelings, especially where God was concerned, may find this difficult. Expressing any kind of feeling toward God other than praise or reverence is deemed by some as a kind of betrayal, a black mark on the church or family crest. For this reason, sometimes when we're angry with God, we've repressed it and we don't even realize it.

Sometimes I'm not interested in prayer because I'm secretly harboring a grudge towards God. It's a secret because I may not even know it myself. I may go several weeks without meaningful prayer, altogether numb to the presence of God. Whether I realize it or not, I'm keeping God at an emotional distance through my resistance to prayer. Most of the time, I'll think that God and I are fine—I just don't have anything I want to say to him. Of course, God knows that I'm not fine. My husband usually does, too.

My husband tells our friends, somewhat comically, that when I say, *"I'm fine,"* and immediately leave the room, he knows he's in trouble. Husbands all across the world, of course, know exactly what this type of behavior is called—the silent treatment. Who was the first wife to discover this tactical maneuver? Who knows, but the silent treatment has been striking fear into the hearts of husbands ever since.

Giving someone the silent treatment is a form of resistance, one that avoids reconciliation through its denial that anything is wrong. When I make a pretense that everything is fine and refuse to "have it out" with my husband, what I'm doing is obvious— I'm keeping the person I love most at an emotional distance. How many of us do that with God, the most loving of all persons? We experience the love of God in a personal way because God is not a concept—God is a person. The biblical God is not the God of the Deists, far removed from us, disengaged with who we are. The biblical God is likewise not the property of scholars—a curiosity to be dissected, deconstructed, stripped of his power and all that he is. Instead, God is the Person most deeply engaged with our lives. If we have arrived at that realization, then without realizing it, we probably relate to God the way that we relate to the people in our lives. It's not that our anger at God, conscious or not, means that God is no longer in our lives. I can tell my husband that I'm fine, get up to unload the dishwasher, go to sleep next to him, wake up the next morning, and go church. We can go through the motions of our day, engage in superficial conversation, and I may never ex- press an active anger. In fact, I may not even know that I'm angry. This can go on for a while, unnoticed by everyone, until suddenly we realize we haven't had a meaningful dinner conversation in weeks. Perhaps our jobs are boring, and there's nothing particularly interesting on the news, so there's nothing much interesting to say. But perhaps, consciously or subconsciously, I don't really feel close to my husband because two weeks ago, he said something that hurt my feelings. We're still in a relationship, we're still doing life together, and I still love him, but there's a breach in our intimacy until I come clean with him about my feelings. For whatever reason, that might be hard for me, or I might not want to do it, or it feels unladylike to raise my voice, or whatever the reason might be. And so we go on existing, never really growing together. Lack of honesty is a hindrance in any relationship, even our relationship with God. It's better to have it out with God than not to talk at all, or to present a cleaned up, edited version of ourselves.

Now don't get me wrong, sometimes editing can be a good thing. This book, for example, desperately needed the skills of a talented editor! Likewise, I often (*kindly, I hope*) beseech my students to edit their work. Editing ourselves can be a good thing when we're tempted to use words that hurt someone else. There, it's often prudent to be mindful about what we say, asking these questions before we respond: *"Is it kind? Is it necessary? It is it true?"* Editing ourselves can also keep us safe when the person we're talking to is, for whatever reason, an unsafe conversation partner. So there are times when editing can be a good thing.

Editing ourselves before God is a different matter altogether. I hear this tendency toward self-editing in conversations with my students when we arrive together at a difficult story in the Bible, or a difficult chapter in their own story: *"Well, everything happens for a reason,"* anger or doubt whittled down to a mere sigh. Lest I be misunderstood here, let me say clearly: I believe that God is good, no matter the wilderness in which I find myself. I believe that God is more than able to convert my pain into his praise. God is more than able to heal my heart *and* to change my circumstances, and if he does neither, God is still good. I'm also not saying that sometimes, our prayers really ought to be reverent. God is, after all, fundamentally different from us. Yet God is not so different from us that he cannot understand the full range of human emotion, even anger.

What I am trying to say, perhaps badly, is this: God never expects us to edit ourselves in his presence. God can take our anger as easily as he can revel in our praise. We need not come before him with a verbal eraser in hand. There we can tell God how it really is, not in pencil markings that can be erased, but confidently, in whatever color pen we like the best. Sometimes in prayer, the color I write in is a peaceful blue because, for a moment, it is well with my soul. In wilderness, however, I might shout my prayers in a fire-engine red because I am mad at God and want to make sure he knows it. And that's okay—God doesn't expect us to be anyone other than who we are. Real prayer is being ourselves before God.

"Being honest with ourselves is a lifelong process," one of my seminary professors once said. Being honest with God is probably a lifelong process, too. Facebook culture has conditioned us to edit ourselves in ways that, undoubtedly, we carry with us into prayer. On social media, most of us post some edited version of the truth about ourselves and our families. Take, for example, a picture of a young couple and their adorable children on Easter. The husband is smiling, appearing thrilled to be wearing whatever pastel-colored outfit his wife picked out, which, incidentally, has been coordinated to match hers. Brother's arm is wrapped around sister. They too are color-coordinated. This picture, practically perfect in every way, may be an accurate depiction of what happened that day. Or, it could be that moments before the picture was taken, the children were squirming, and the husband was complaining that he hated it when his wife asked him to wear a tie. The perfect picture captured on Facebook does not reveal the stress it took to get everybody to stand still, the eye-rolling of the kids that they had to wear nice clothes, or the tension on the car ride to church. There's the truth, and then there's the picture that suggests that everything is great, all the time. Is it possible for everything to be great, all the time? Of course not.

Likewise, it is impossible for everything to be great, all the time, in our relationship with God. The reality is that sometimes our relationship with God reads like a Facebook status itself: *"It's complicated, with God."* Presenting too cheery a picture of ourselves and our relationship with God in prayer hinders our prayer, likely indicating we haven't gotten too deep with God in the first place. Like any relationship that really matters, prayer is simultaneously the easiest thing we ever do, and the hardest. But we keep on showing up for it, because talking—or yelling—things out is how we grow, even in our relationship with God. And so when I went out on my back deck that November morning to really let God have it, I yelled at him about the "stuck" nature of my wilderness.

I also yelled at God because I was hungry and thirsty for the life I used to know. The Israelites voice this same complaint: "We remember the fish we used to eat in Egypt for nothing, the cucumbers, the melons, the leeks, the onions, and the garlic; but now our strength is dried up, and there is nothing at all but this manna to look at" (Num 11:5–6 NRSV). It's hard to imagine daydreaming about melons and leeks, but there are plenty of my own creature comforts that I miss. Sometimes on our way to the farmer's market on a lazy Saturday, my husband and I play a little car game. *"You know what would be great right now?"* I say. *"A cappuccino from O'Henry's."* O'Henry's Coffee is in Homewood, Alabama, nowhere near the farmer's market in Waco, but that doesn't stop me from daydreaming about it. And it's impossible for me to be present to my surroundings because I'm daydreaming of home. Prayer is like that. Sometimes, we're just not interested in God because, rightly or wrongly, we've got other things on our mind. O'Henry's cappuccino is delicious and, sometimes by comparison, the life God has provided in Waco doesn't seem nearly as sweet.

Hunger and thirst for the life we used to know acknowledges that some kind of "leave-taking" has happened. All the markers of the life we used to know are gone. "Way," as the Quakers called it, has closed. In the wilderness, yes, "Way" closes, but in the wilderness, the rest of the world opens up. If we have the eyes to see it, the barrenness of the wilderness is a gift. With its stark terrain, the wilderness is just desolate enough to for us to see our lives truthfully, with all the underbrush cleared away. It is a severe form of grace, certainly, but it is grace just the same. With baptized eyes and with sanctified ears, all of a sudden, we come to realize that we can no longer treat prayer like a monologue. Prayer is instead a conversation. And if prayer is a conversation and not a monologue, sooner or later, we ought to be prepared for God to *speak back*.

What I imagine God saying to us in the wilderness is what I also imagine him saying to the Israelites: "*Yell all you want,*" God says. "*But trust that what I give you is enough.*"

And all of a sudden, there it is—manna—fallen like grace onto the dry ground of our lives. Named for its very "whatness," at first the Israelites don't know what it is when they see it (Exod 16:14–15). Biblical scholars claim manna looked like a flaky, liquidy substance, maybe like Cream of Wheat. If you've ever scoured the pantry for a midnight snack, you know that box of Cream of Wheat tucked away on the bottom shelf isn't usually what you reach for. Sometimes, manna is like that: we know that it's nourishing, we know that it's good for us, we know it's a gift, and still we don't want it. Like the Israelites, most of us would probably rather have meat (*okay, chocolate . . .*) than manna. You may want one thing, but God has provided another thing. God has put whatever manna he has put into our pantries, and regardless of how it tastes, manna is always grace. Like grace, we have to be humble enough to stoop low and pick it up, or stoop low and pull it from the bottom shelf. Bending low to receive what God gives us is one of the hardest things we ever do in the wilderness. But as Richard Rohr once said, our rest is in what God gives us, not in a particular outcome.

The manna probably looks different for us during different wilderness seasons. During my doctoral work in New Jersey, a wilderness season eerily similar to the wilderness of Waco, manna came through discovering the writings of spiritual writer Henri Nouwen. Henri became my spiritual director and prayer partner. Every Saturday, I took Henri with me on long walks outside the quaint town of Chatham, New Jersey. We walked together, sat together in a café over coffee and dessert, and I lingered over every word of his books, not wanting them to end. In that same season, manna came through two different jobs, one at a church and another at a grocery store. In other seasons, manna has looked like an invitation to sit on my pastor's sofa while he listened with me to my life, or school breaks in my grandmother's Tennessee mountain home. Most often in my life, manna has come through people who saw me struggling and offered grace. And that's the thing about manna, it always come through a Person, Jesus. Ultimately, the manna God has given to is himself (John 6:22–51).

So when I went out on my back deck to yell at God on that crisp, November morning, I knew I wasn't really done with God. Not by a long shot. How could I be? We can think we're mad enough or sad enough to be totally done with God, but God gets the final say in these kinds of thing.

"Yell all you want," God says, with a chuckle. *"But I'm not going anywhere."*

4

Smashing Idols

My experience as a Bible teacher to women in a drug and alcohol rehabilitation center was brief, but memorable. For a year, I regularly drove twenty minutes from my home in the suburbs of Birmingham to what felt like a totally different part of the world. If I forgot momentarily that I was on the wrong side of the tracks, the catcalls I heard from men I did not know as I walked to the building were a quick reminder.

My job was to teach basic Bible for women in the program, many of whom had been abused, sold into prostitution, or incarcerated. All of them were addicts. Some were in rehabilitation for the first time, many were not. My class was held in the basement in a windowless room with heavy desks that screeched when they were moved across the concrete floor. Every time I entered that room to teach them, I did so with trembling knees, aware that I was entering both a holy ground and a battleground.

I have no personal experience of rehab myself, except for the year I spent as a guest among these women whose stories I would come to know. To say that the experience was pleasant would be to misrepresent it. It was not pleasant—it was difficult work in an environment that differed in every way from my own privileged background, as well as from the privileged background of the students I was used to teaching. Years removed from that experience now, what I can say about it is that I will never be the same: it opened up my faith in ways that teaching in my usual context never could. I was a better teacher there than anywhere else I have ever taught.

What I discovered was that rehab is itself a kind of wilderness experience. An uncomfortable in-between space, one that stretches past enslavement to your drug or god of choice, but a space that highlights you are not yet free. I imagine that the temptation to relapse is something akin to the temptation to return to Egypt, to return to what you know, to serve the gods who have, in their own perverse way, served you until you begin to break free of them, mustering all the strength you have until you make it, momentarily, to wilderness, or to rehab, a place of temporary rest. Yet like the wilderness, rehab is not only a place of rest. Like the wilderness, rehab is also a place where you come face to face with God—both the false god who brought you here and the God who is actually here, offering to set you free.

I didn't put any of this together at first. In the beginning, most of my reflection centered on how I could maintain control of the classroom. Loud side conversations between students, frequent, distracting questions about things unrelated to the topic (*like who I was dating at the time: Keith Urban, I said*), and screeching desks across the concrete floor, were all part of the classroom cacophony I had to adjust to as we made our way through the Old Testament.

A couple of months went by as I adjusted to teaching in this context. Somewhere in the middle of that, I had something of my own intervention, and it came to me in a dream. It wasn't a particularly unusual or interesting day when I went home after work, went to bed, and woke up from a vivid dream.

"I have a job for you to do," a blurry, faceless man said. *"I need you to tell my people about Egypt."*

And just like that, it was over. It was a perplexing dream, but by the next day I had forgotten all about it. About a week went by, and in class we had arrived at the story of the Israelites and the golden calf. It is a familiar story for many of us, one we usually pull out in Sunday school to illustrate our collective tendencies to worship false gods. In the story, the Israelites have just been freed from slavery in Egypt and have found themselves in the wilderness, waiting to go to the promised land.

The Israelites don't last long in the wilderness before they get fed up with this God who isn't so keen on showing his face. Hebrew theology stipulated that no one could look upon the face of God and live. If Moses, that man most intimately acquainted with God, had to be shielded from God's face even as he received the Ten Commandments, then the Israelites weren't likely to get a good look at God, either (Exod 33:12–23). So there the Israelites stood, at the base of Mount Sinai, the holiest of mountains in biblical tradition, while the conversation between God and Moses dragged on for over a month. Left to their own devices, the Israelites create a false god to worship—with poor, stupid Aaron exclaiming: *"These are your gods, O Israel, who brought you up out of the land of Egypt!"* (Exod 32:4, 8 NRSV).

It would be a comical scene if it wasn't such a tragic one.

Aaron comes off like a child caught standing in the kitchen with mud everywhere, face and shoes covered in it, futilely attempting to pin the whole thing on the dog.

"You know how these people are," Aaron tells Moses. "They're so bad. You see, what happened was that they took off all their jewelry, I threw it in the fire, and out popped this golden calf!" (Exod 32:24).

Aaron's comical cover story aside, there's a sadness to the scene that resonated deeply with the addicts I was teaching. They began to compare the false gods the Israelites worshipped to their own false gods—their drugs of choice. As they began to share their stories, suddenly I felt I was on holy ground. Looking down, the concrete floor began to feel like *humus*, the Latin for earth or ground, where we get our word *humility*.

The wilderness is like that—it teaches you humility. You begin to look down, down to the concrete floor that screeches whenever the desks are moved across it, a groaning sound, I imagine, not unlike the whole world as it travails under its own suffering. Look down to the earth, recognize the *humus* from which you've come, and know that you are dust. And when you search deep down,

down under the earth of your own humiliation, you discover your god of choice buried there. Your god might be just beneath the soil, or it might take a shovel and rope to dig it out from underneath all that Christian piety and your Jesus-y right answers, but it's there. And so you look down, so that you can eventually look up—so that you can hold to the fluorescent light, the one always threatening to flicker off in that windowless basement room, the truth of your life.

The light can flicker off just as quickly as it flickered on, so bring your whole life into its purview while the bulb is still lit and the earth still gives way. And what you find there, when you lift it to the light, is not buried treasure—but buried pain, and with it, whatever imagined picture of God who has accompanied you there.

Just like us, the Israelites used their imaginations to create many different pictures of God. Consequently, there are lots of different words for "image" in the Old Testament. In the story of the Israelites and the golden calf, the Hebrew word is *Massekah*, an image cast out of metal. These images could be contorted into whatever shape the Israelites wanted to make—in this case, a calf, symbolic of fertility in the ancient world. Throughout the Old Testament, a *Massekah* is a negative image, a perversion of who God is and what God looks like. Maybe that's one reason the Israelites are told *not* to make an image of God—we're bound to get it wrong. The Israelites don't know enough about God yet to have much of a clue about what he looks like.

Now, to be fair, the Israelites hadn't journeyed with God long before he went missing. With God calling Moses, the only representation the people have of God and of what God wants, up to the mountain, the Israelites are left on their own to do their theological homework. Clearly, they aren't ready for that. It's too soon in the seminary curriculum to leave them totally alone, so God leaves Aaron, the lesser of the two teaching assistants, at the bottom of that fiery mountain, probably hoping for the best. It's obvious that Aaron isn't much further along in the seminary curriculum than the rest of that sorry lot, because he helps them contort the curvatures of the good, liberating God who had brought them out of slavery, into cast images, perverted things. And the next day, they make sacrifices to the images of the gods they made. In making those sacrifices, the people sacrifice a piece of themselves, too.

It is an inescapable reality that our theologies and our anthropologies are intertwined. How we view God has implications for how view ourselves and others, too. Bad theology not only contorts a beautiful, good God into an ugly thing—it distorts our own faces as well. Whenever we worship an image of God that is false, we lose a little piece of ourselves. When we look in the mirror, we better make darn sure we're wearing a good pair of glasses. Because whatever image we see reflected back at ourselves is one rooted in whatever it is we imagine to be true about God.

You shall have no other gods besides me, God tells the Israelites (Exod 20:3; Deut 5:7). When God puts an "s" on the end of "gods," I don't think that's any accident. Come to find out, lots of gods—or images of god—turn up in the wilderness.

Whatever your image of god is, you'll probably find a community to worship it with you. The Israelites worshipped in community, and so do we. We too divide ourselves into "camps," places of ideological safety where we take shelter under the unquestioned assumption that we are right. We live, work, and worship among those who think and look like we do, creating ideological enemies out of those who live in a different "camp" than we do. The ancient Israelites believed that God *must* dwell exclusively in their territory, or they would be destroyed. Turns out, we're not so different. God forbid that God also dwell with the people who think differently from us. In our fractious age, social media is either an echo chamber or a place to wage our ideological wars against the "other," whoever that is. Like the ancient Israelites, Christians also divide themselves into camps, places where we hang on for dear life to our image(s) of God.

God is the One who supports tightening our borders.

No, God wants us to be magnanimous towards those coming in.

God doesn't want us to drink alcohol.

41

Nah, God's down at the local brewery right now, where I lead my small group.

And on and on it goes.

In graduate school, I was introduced to the Jewish theologian Martin Buber, who said that the Israelites were told not to make an image of God because it was simply impossible to capture all that God is in one image.

"You shall not make an image," Buber said, *"which means at the same time, you can't make an image."*

I suppose I agree with Buber, but for a different reason—whenever I make an image of God, that image is bound to look like me. That god will vote how I vote, take his coffee the same way I take it, and be grumpy about the same things I'm grumpy about.

Anne Lamott said it best: *"You can safely assume you've created God in your own image when it turns out that God hates all the same people you do."*[1]

Right on, Anne.

But here's the thing—just because we shouldn't make images of God—or can't make images of God—doesn't mean we don't try.

All our images of God are *formed* somehow—we create them out of our pain, our longing, our desire to live on our own terms. So unearth that false image, take a good long look at it, and then let it go. And climb up that mountain, searching for the God who truly is, the One who has loved you before you were born and who will go on loving you after you die.[2] Find that God, because he's hidden in the wilderness, too. In the wilderness, pulling out that false god you've buried below the earth and holding it up to the fluorescent light in whatever windowless, basement room you find yourself—well, that's an act of humility. Addicts call it surrender.

I'm embarrassed to admit it, but one of the images of god I'm learning to surrender is the image of a god who wants me to be comfortable. It's a god whose name I never said aloud, to myself or to anyone else. I'm ashamed to know this pay-to-play god was in my pantheon, but he was there, with an avaricious appetite,

1. Lamott, *Bird by Bird*, 22.
2. Nouwen, *Finding My Way Home*.

ungrateful and always wanting more. Wearing a killer outfit from Ann Taylor Loft, jamming to the latest girl power anthem song, and swigging a five-dollar cappuccino, that god had health/wealth gospel written all over his sorry face. He was the kind of god we learned to snicker at in seminary and to rip apart in our sermons. He was the kind of god who was dangerous to the good-hearted folks who sat in the pews, struggling to trust God was with them and also struggling to pay their bills on time. He was the god who promised all the shiny things, all happiness all the time, if you just praised him loudly enough. That god wasn't hard to find. Turns out, I had left him in the wilderness, somewhere just south of a rock and a hard place.

And like Peter when he denies Jesus in the Gospels, I wept bitterly when I turned and saw the real God standing in front of me. We always wind up weeping bitterly when we find ourselves worshipping the wrong god. The apostle Paul would later call that godly sorrow, and it's the kind of sorrow leading you all the way to rehab, where you hopefully get your repentance right, letting go of whatever is your god of choice.

I suppose it's some comfort that even Jesus' own disciples served this god from time to time. Those adorable sons of Zebedee, disciples of Jesus, had a mama that, God love her, just thought her boys were the bee's knees. "When it's all over and the kingdom finally comes, can my boys sit, one at your right, and one at your left? Can they have a more prominent position than everybody else?" (Matt 20:21).

Bless her heart, as we say in the South.

With a mama like that, it's no wonder her boys, along with the rest of the disciples, found themselves consistently jockeying for position.

"What were you arguing about back there?" Jesus asked the disciples (Mark 9:33–37).

The disciples wouldn't fess up, so the narrator decided to tattle on them: "But they were silent, for on the way they had argued about who was the greatest" (Mark 9:34).

Ouch.

Jesus responds to these impositions by serving up a dose of humble pie, as we say in the South. I'm not quite sure what ingredients you buy at the store to make humble pie—I just know it doesn't taste so good.

If you're in the story already, you can probably smell the humble pie cooking a mile away.

And apple pie à la mode, it ain't.

Jesus places a child in between them, telling them that they should imitate the child.

Ouch.

"Can you drink the cup that I'm going to drink?" Jesus later asks (Matt 20:22; Mark 10:38).

Like naïve, overly confident seminarians, those poor disciples lift up their shoulders, flex their tiny muscles, and say, "We can" (Matt 20:22).

"Oh, you'll drink my cup all right, but you won't be sitting at my right or at my left" (Matt 20:23).

Ouch.

Would you like your humble pie served à la mode, or not?

The disciples had to rehab, to restore, their view of who God was and what he wanted for them.

So did I.

I'm not quite sure how I missed it, after all this time, but the "position" God puts us in is not one of personal comfort. God positions us to drink the cup that he drinks, to carry the cross, and to die to ourselves.

I knew all that already, but something about being in the wilderness exposed the false god I had been serving.

It's a hard truth, but here it is: after I do all the right things, I shouldn't expect much of anything in return. Just acknowledging that I am a humble servant of God, doing only what God has asked me to, nothing unique or special about it (Luke 17:10). A relationship with God is not about being friends with benefits—it's about being friends. True friendship with God means walking the way that Jesus walked—to the cross, or to the wilderness. Pick your metaphor, I guess, but this is a book mostly about wilderness.

All this worrying about position or image, especially in our Christian culture—it's death to the soul. That's not what life with God is about. I'm still learning that.

I'll be learning it until the day I die.

The wilderness is the school where I learn it.

The god promising me that if I really loved God, I'd never find myself in wilderness—or that I deserved happiness because I loved God—I unearthed him there. I think it's a safe bet to say that the Israelites also unearthed that same god in the wilderness—otherwise, they wouldn't find themselves yelling at God so much about wanting to go back to Egypt.

As it turns out, there are lots of images of God who turn up in the wilderness. I carved this first image out of my own selfishness. Theologians call it *in curvatus se*, to be turned in on the self (*that's about the best definition of "sin" I've ever heard, by the way*).

Another image of God I uncovered in the wilderness I had created, quite simply, out of pain. While I was digging around in the dirt, I stumbled across the god that accused me of wickedness, who always found something wrong with me. That god said I was in the wilderness because I had done something wrong. That god was there too, and boy, that little sucker caused me a lot of heartache. Somehow, he crept into my pantheon, even though I knew better than to let him in. In my experience, this god usually creeps in when we're feeling especially vulnerable. And oh man, there's nothing like wilderness to make you feel vulnerable.

It was on a particularly vulnerable day that I sat across from my spiritual director to make this confession: "*I feel like maybe God is mad at me. We don't feel as close as we used to, and I've noticed that I've been avoiding him. Recently, I felt really cared for by God, really seen by him, but now I feel like I'm just too wicked, too ungrateful, for him to want to be with me. I feel like maybe he's mad at me. Or maybe it's that I'm mad at me. I'm not sure which it is.*"

It was one of those moments when you know if you utter just one more syllable, you'll dissolve into tears. With a lump in my throat, I stopped talking, waiting for her response, needing to catch my breath.

As a trained spiritual director myself, there are certain words that I've been taught to notice. "Wicked" is certainly one of them. She was right to draw my attention to my use of that word.

"Wicked?" she said. *"Where do you think that view of yourself comes from? You're God's child. Do you think you might spend some time restoring your image of God? I think that would be good, meaningful work for you to do."*

The image of God, the *imago Dei*—we encounter this idea at the very start of things, all the way back to Genesis 1. There we read about how God created a good world and an especially good humanity. Genesis 1:26–27 uses the word *tselem* for "image," a word closely related to the idea of a "shadow." We are patterned and formed, these verses say, in God's image. We reflect his shadow. And when we stand among shadows of divinity, what we find is an inherently good God, a God of love. The whole Bible, from cover to cover, affirms this. Patterned after this God of love, we too are stitched together by invisible threads of love and goodness.

I can imagine that some of you are thinking, *"What about original sin?"* Sure, I get you. "Original sin" comes to us by way of the church father Augustine, and I have nothing against the guy. Well, maybe his ideas about women weren't so great (*boyfriend could have worked out his mommy issues in therapy, but I digress* . . .). From Augustine, we inherit the interpretation of Genesis 1–3 that humankind is inherently depraved, inherently, "originally" sinful. This is the view of humanity that much of Western Christianity adopts, baptizes over time as the standard anthropology, the accepted understanding of humankind.

Here's the deal—I know I'm a sinner. Ask my students, ask my friends, ask my husband—while you're at it, ask my cat. They'll all tell you that I'm a sinner, and I'd heartily agree with them. Except for the dog—I don't care what he thinks. But I'm not *just* a sinner, and neither are you. Before we were ever sinners, we were beloved children, created in the image of God. That's the fundamental truth of who we are. When we take Augustine's anthropology too far, we lose sight of the original pattern—we were created in the image of a good and beloved Creator. This inherently good, creative, loving God, patterned us after himself. We reflect his shadow. If we only see God as One who is always pointing fingers at us, who is critiquing every word we say, every bad haircut we get, all the times we could have said something nice to that annoying guy in the pew across from us, then we'll only see ourselves as wicked. And, the only image of God we'll ever see is One who is always fault-finding. Our theology and our anthropology go hand in hand—one informs the other. The restoration of our image of God into a loving Creator also restores our image of ourselves as beloved children of God. We may never find our way to a rehab center, but at one point or another, we come face-to-face with our god of choice. And, it's there where we are given a choice—either rehab that image and find the God who loves us, or let that god of choice, the one we've created, continue to cause us pain.

The same good God who made a good world and everything in it, is the same God who brought the Israelites out of slavery, yearning with them for a better life. A God who hears the cry of the oppressed, a God who sees both the individual and the community, a God who would, in the figure of Jesus, enter the homes of both the self-righteous and those who were actually righteous—that's the same God who's nestled behind burning bushes, advocating for the people on Mount Sinai, and who holds lanterns and flashlights to guide your way through the darkest places. The God who's with you when everything's going right, is the same God who's with you when your whole world has fallen apart. The God of the good places is the God of the hard places, too. God is the same God, whether he feels close, visible to you, or devastatingly invisible.

I am a twenty-first-century Christian living much removed from ancient Hebrew culture. One thing I share with the Hebrew people of long ago, however, is that I love a God who is invisible, hidden. The longer I have walked with this God, the less I am befuddled by this. I have come to recognize him, hidden in plain sight. I have come to recognize the curvatures of his face, nestled in the crevices of the crinkled eyes of the ones who love me well. I have come to hear his voice, largely inaudible, in words that are true and good and holy, spoken or sung by those who have learned to listen to him. I have come to fall in love with the shape of him, in the shapes of all the bodies—black, white, and brown, large and small, young and old, who embody his goodness and love. When I look at the people all around me in this good world that God has made, I find that God is not so invisible after all.

5

The Great Silence

It was a question that must have jolted him from a deep sleep:

"What are you doing here, Elijah?" (1 Kgs 19:9, 13).

Already a day's journey into the wilderness and exhausted to the point of death, Elijah had fallen asleep, but not before laying out his grievances to God—*just go ahead and kill me* (1 Kgs 19:4). Instead of giving Elijah what he asked for, God asked him one of those really big questions, the kind that each of us has to answer if we're ever going to move out of whatever place it is in which we're stuck. And of course, God knows what we're doing here, just as God knew what Elijah was doing in that wilderness all by himself, wanting to die. No, God doesn't ask questions for his own benefit, and even if he did, heaven knows, God is himself the answer to every question. But the question had come, and suddenly Elijah found himself in a conversation about his own life with that most familiar of strangers, God. This is a God who decides when and how he will speak, and Elijah is given a choice about how he will respond.

It was somewhere in the middle of the fourth year of my own wilderness that Elijah's question became my question. I turned the page to Elijah's story and read it, as if for the first time. I received the question, *"What are you doing here?"* with an alarming kinship and a surprising empathy, because it was the same question I had begun to pose to myself: *"What are you doing here, Noel?"*

The answer came, oddly, in a dream: *"You are in Waco to die to yourself."*

It was an odd dream, but not unexpected. That particular year, death had already wrapped itself around me like a heavy blanket. It was winter, and I had returned to a familiar place, the small room at Sumatanga where we gather for worship. At week's end, it is our tradition to join hands in a circle and to sing our goodbyes before returning home. Since we are all over the country, these are our last moments together, with three long months before we meet again. Joining our voices together in singing "Song of Shalom" has become one of the most meaningful traditions of our shared experience. Love is evident around that circle. As we look into each other's faces, many of us have tears in our eyes. That afternoon, however, what I felt was not *shalom*, peace, but something altogether different—panic.

As I glanced around the circle of happy faces—the faces of people I had come to love—suddenly, I felt all alone. I looked down at my feet to make sure I was still standing, because I felt weightless. I knew my lips were moving as I sung those familiar words, but I couldn't hear them. What I heard instead, as though whispered from someplace outside myself, were questions that frightened me.

Does my life make any difference?

Would it matter to anyone if I just disappeared?

Do I want to be here anymore, at all?

Two weeks later, I was in a counselor's office, joined by my husband. He held my hand as my counselor said words I'll never forget: *"I hear you using words like 'disappear' and 'gone,' and sometimes we use words like those when we can't bring ourselves to say what we really mean. When you say you wish you could disappear, do you really mean you wish you were dead?"*

I nodded, unable to speak.

Together, the three of us created a crisis prevention plan, something I had never heard of. If a crisis situation arose, I could call my counselor, my husband, or the two friends whose numbers I had been instructed to write down. Dutifully, I wrote down the phone numbers of two friends I have known for twenty years, but I was too ashamed to tell them about it. I was also instructed to think about tangible times in my life when I had been happy, in order to counter the other things I might feel in a moment of crisis. We brainstormed together in the office about what those memories might be, and my brain was in such a fog that I couldn't think.

The rest of that day remains a blur. I felt so deeply tired. That afternoon in the counselor's office was one of the worst days of my life (*now two years later, I can't say that I'm totally whole, or happy, or out of that particular wilderness just yet, but I do have people that can help wrap me in a blanket of love when death begins to hover too closely*).

It's a heavy word—*death*—and it frightens me even now thinking that I had come to that place. I had spent three years yelling at God, waiting for him to bring us out of this wilderness, and now I was so tired that I wanted to die. As the months rolled back, the moments when I wanted to die seemed to outnumber the moments when I wanted to keep going. There are people who live much of their lives wishing they had never been born. I grieved for those people, until that day around the circle at Sumatanga, I realized that I was one of them. I also realized that the love of God was no longer a warm sweater that I could wrap around myself during a winter of pain. I loved God—knew that I did—and still I wanted to die. It was a place I never thought I'd find myself.

It was a place, I'm sure, no one else envisioned for me either. Strangely, one of the things that grieved me most was how dishonest it all felt. I was the person who offered spiritual care to my students. I sat with them while they cried, rejoiced with them in happy times, and prayed with them during the spaces in between. If they knew the person who had walked alongside them in these personal ways was struggling so deeply, they would have been shocked. I felt ashamed by the vast divide between my public face and my private pain. I had never felt so dishonest in my whole life. I had been out in this wilderness too long—tired, lonely, and unable to hear God.

When I read the story where Elijah tells God that he wants to die, in my own way, I understand.

In the midst of Elijah's distress, God instructs Elijah to wait for him at Mount Horeb, the mountain of God. Horeb is the same mountain where, as the Israelites tell it, God first revealed himself to Moses. It is the same place sanctified in the imagination of the Israelites, who repeat the same old story year after year: God heard us, and God acted. After all that time enslaved in Egypt, God broke the silence and offered us a word. In fact, God didn't just offer us *a word*—God gave us *all the words*, 613 commandments, to be exact. Before Elijah ever gets there, this mountain has already been sanctified as a place where God meets God's people.

So poor, tired Elijah straps on his Nikes, powers off his iPod, and musters whatever is left of his strength to trudge up that old mountain to wait for God, worn out and uncertain if he'll hear much of anything at all. What he heard at first was a whole lot of noise that amounted to a whole lot of nothing.

And after the noise had died down, silence (1 Kgs 19:12b).

The great mystic Meister Eckhart put it beautifully—*There is nothing in all Creation so like God as stillness.*

If I may, allow me to put it this way: *Silence is another name for God.*

We need look no further than Genesis 1 to encounter *Silence*. In the story of the world's unfolding—and of the unfolding relationship between God and humankind—the narrative tells us that there was *something before all the words*. That *something* is really *Someone*—*Silence, God*, dark and gestating.

The writer of Genesis 1, poet that he was, describes the scene: a formless earth, churning, chaotic waters, and silence. The earth was *tohu vbohu*, which means a trackless waste—just like a wilderness. Later on, the prophets use this same phrase to describe the experience of the Israelites in exile from their homeland—it too was like a wilderness (Isa 34:11; Jer 4:23). And, it too felt like a place where God was often silent. Still, I don't think Isaiah and Jeremiah, those great men of God who bemoaned the state of affairs of God's people, viewed the *tohu vbohu* as wasted space.

The moments in the dark and in the silence just prior to creation, like the time spent in the wilderness of exile, are the pauses, the breaths, before a new word can be spoken. Before something new can be born. Before life.

Creation was not alone in the waiting—the breath of God silently hovered over the waters. It was quiet enough, I imagine, not just to hear it—but to feel it. To feel the presence of God lingering there. Likewise, the Israelites were not alone in the wilderness, and later, they were not alone in exile—the presence of God tabernacled with them. And likewise, Elijah was not alone when he was waiting at that mountain, half wanting to hear God, half just wanting to die. We are not alone in the waiting, either. God enters into the Great Silence with us.

In fact, among the medieval mystics, one beautiful strand of Christian theology, *God is the Great Silence.*

And the Great Silence is the One who waits with us in the spaces between death and new life.

It is so easy to mistake silence for something that it is not. Too often, we mistake God's silence for God's anger over our sinfulness, or God's disinterest, or God's lack of compassion toward us.

Life with God is one long conversation, and there are words. Sometimes lots and lots of words. And then there are the pauses between the words where we sit with what has been said. Those pauses are called "silence," and they are a natural cadence of conversation. The Great Silence in between all the words allows the soul to wait, to rest, to process, and this Great Silence cannot be hurried.

God is the Great Silence, and every time we enter into it, our soul enters into God.

> The soul is like a wild animal—tough, resilient, savvy, self-sufficient and yet exceedingly shy. If we want to see a wild animal, the last thing we should do is to go crashing through the woods, shouting for the creature to come out. But when we are willing to walk quietly into the woods and sit silently for an hour or two at the base of a tree, the creature we are waiting for may well emerge, and out of the corner of an eye we will catch a glimpse of what we seek.[1]

1. Palmer, *Hidden Wholeness*, 58.

There is a truth that only the soul can tell, but that truth will emerge only when the soul is ready to tell it. Until then, we wait and allow Silence to pull up a chair. We welcome Silence, like a friend, offering to it all the grace in the world because we trust that all this waiting will be worth it. We trust that in the waiting, new life is unfolding.

It is one of the great blessings of my life that waiting and listening is part of my vocation. As a person who teaches university and seminary students for a living, much of what I do involves listening with students as their lives unfold. This often involves a lot of fits and starts—sometimes a lot of noise that's a whole lot of nothing—and sometimes a lot of silence that leads to new beginnings.

In the times when I forget that silence is part of the conversation, I grow impatient when my students remain silent in class. Suddenly, I find myself on the metaphorical mountaintop (*near the lectern in the classroom*), lonely and confused, waiting for my partner in this shared conversation to speak. On days like that, I feel like all I am doing is speaking into the air—my words only blustering winds, noisy placeholders, for when my conversation partner has gone silent. It is so easy to mistake Silence for something that it is not—anger, fear, disinterest, mistrust.

Not long ago, I spent an entire semester befuddled by the silence of a particular class I was teaching. The students were kind people, I think. They were so quiet that it was hard to tell. They smiled politely, they answered a question occasionally, laughed respectfully (*probably out of reverential pity*) at the jokes I told. But mostly, they were so . . . silent. I sifted through any number of reasons why they may have been silent, perhaps none of them true. An entire semester came and went, the grades were posted, and I never solved the mystery. At the end of the semester, those same students offered many kind, reassuring words on my teaching evaluation. Nothing had appeared to go wrong.

And then one day out of the blue, one of those students dropped by my office to offer a surprising word: "*I loved your class. Thank you for giving me the space to be silent this semester. I think*

I'm in a season of listening right now, trying to figure out who I'm becoming. Keeping quiet is helping me to listen. I'm grateful you didn't force me to speak until I was ready. Thank you for welcoming my silence."

Her words were simple yet profound. Like the prophet Elijah, she too had sat in a wilderness cave of sorts, waiting for the Lord to pass by. It was a good reminder to me—we must not force those who are not yet ready to speak. To do so would be to enact a particular sort of violence on those who are vulnerable to our many words.

It is so easy to mistake Silence for things that it is not—anger, fear, disinterest, mistrust.

And so we welcome the Great Silence, like a friend, offering to him all the grace in the world because we trust that all this waiting will be worth it.

God is the Great Silence.

After all this time I've spent with God—my whole life, really—what I can say is this: God is worth the wait. God's silence is like my student's silence—there's a bit of mystery to it. There may be any number of reasons why God is silent, but, oh my God, I just know God is worth the wait. When we understand that whatever it is we're waiting for is not *Something* but *Someone*, we understand, truly, what it is to come home. What it is to welcome the Silence.

That doesn't mean that the waiting is easy, or painless. As I later discovered, there were layers of pain nestled beneath my student's silence. There are layers of pain, tucked like scarves around all our necks. Waiting for God to speak is no easy thing, especially when there's no knock on our door alerting us to God's painful past and God's offer of thanks for welcoming the silence. Especially when there's no end-of-the-semester evaluation, telling us that everything, actually, is just fine. There's a loneliness to the waiting. Profoundly, deeply felt, thick layers of mist on the frosted, leaf-crackled ground of the soul. We better not make too much noise, though, lest we scare away a soul in process. Still, there's a loneliness to the waiting.

I sometimes wonder if God feels lonely while he's waiting for me.

This is of course one of those great theological questions: Does God feel things? Can God suffer—suffer in the same ways that we do? Suffer emotionally, experience loneliness, anger, sadness, jealousy, the spectrum of human emotion? Some believe that he can't. I believe that he can, and that he does.

Famously, St. Teresa of Avila said that God didn't have too many friends. Possibly, that's true. While I sometimes bewail the silence on the other end of my prayers, I wonder if God mourns my own silence. I wonder if God feels lonely while he's waiting for me. I don't know *that* he does—but I wonder *if* he does.

What I do know is this: *whatever* it is that God feels, that feeling is holy. Because whatever else we might say about God, God is holy, and whatever God touches is holy, too. If God feels lonely, then there's a holiness to God's loneliness, and if God has touched the place of my own loneliness, then that loneliness has been made holy, too. When God touches the ground of our waiting, then that place is holy.

There is a holiness to the waiting, and that holiness is held together by that most familiar of strangers—God, and God's love. And so it is Love—that one most acquainted with suffering and with grief—who meets us in the place of our deepest loneliness, the ground of our waiting. And if we have enough strength to bend our ear low enough to the ground and hear just one thing whispered to us out of all that Silence, may it be this: what we are waiting for is not *Something*, but *Someone*.

He is the Someone for whom all of us waits, whether we know it or not. And as that mystic Carlo Carretto said, God comes like the sun in the morning—when it is time.[2]

God is that One, both familiar and strange—closer than our next breath, yet by his own admission, a God who hides himself too (Isa 45:15; 54:8). His is the Voice we listen for in a hundred different places, whose face we look for on a hundred different faces. That Someone, that familiar stranger, is God.

2. Carretto, *God Who Comes*, 28.

God is the Great Silence.

And God breaks his silence like the breath exhaling over the waters at creation—when it is time.

And when the Great Silence breaks and his presence is exhaled, there we find ourselves at Genesis once more—at a new beginning.

My new beginning came, as so many new beginnings do come, as a kind of ending: *"You are in Waco to die to yourself,"* I heard in a dream during that season when death seemed to hover all around me and I didn't know if I would make it out of the wilderness alive.

Before something new can be born, something else has to die, and that something is our vision for the way things are.

That something else is the self.

And once we stop listening to the noise of our own understanding,[3] to the self and to what it wants, we enter into the Great Silence.

The Great Silence—it breathed over the waters at creation, it exhaled on Elijah on the mountain, and it was, I imagine, a weighty presence in a darkened tomb just before Jesus was resurrected.

God is the Great Silence.

And if we bend our ears just low enough to the ground, that Great Silence teaches us that death isn't the only thing that happens in the wilderness.

Resurrection happens there, too, and God waits with us for it.

---

3. Mulholland, *Shaped by the Word*, 55.

6

Naming God

THE NAME OF THE well was *Beer-lahai-roi*, which means "The Well of the Living One Who Sees Me." The name of the woman weeping beside the well was *Hagar*, whose name means "the Stranger," "the Wanderer," or "the Resident Alien." None of these names exactly rolls off the tongue. The only part of the name *Beer-lahai-roi* that I'm absolutely certain how to pronounce is *"Beer,"* and I'm pretty sure the biblical author and I don't have the same thing in mind. Still, names—and naming experiences—are an important part of this story. Names are an important part of my story, too.

All my life, I have gone by my middle name, Noel. While it was clear early in the pregnancy that I was going to be a girl, my parents decided to name me John, after my father. My mother decided on my middle name, so the story goes, long before I was ever born, when she saw it displayed on an ornament at Christmastime. She had thought briefly about naming me "Hope," but once she saw that ornament, the name "Noel" stuck.

I've always had a complicated relationship with my name. As a child at school, whenever the teacher called the name "John" on the roll, I answered *"Here,"* in a tiny, female voice, amidst the snickers of my peers. Inevitably, I was met by the confused face of an otherwise kind teacher. And, inevitably, I responded by asking to be called by my middle name. I dreaded the first day of school each year.

Over the years, I tried as much as I could to distance my-self from the name John, but its always stuck. Official documents, voter registration, marriage license—the name is still there. Most of the time, I try to pretend like the TSA agent who's checking my passport is the first person who's ever made a joke about it. People like to be original, so usually I try to play along. Plus, it's never wise to get too snarky with the TSA. When I got married, I thought briefly about changing my name, but somehow that felt like a family betrayal, so, for better or for worse, in sickness and in health, I'm named for life.

There are days when I'm actually glad about it. As much as I've tried to distance myself from the name John, it is a reminder of all the good characteristics I've inherited from my father. A life-long runner and forty years my senior, that man can still outpace me on the running trail. He's the hardest worker I know, with a stubbornness that is, mostly, a good thing.

About the time I entered doctoral work, I needed to be re-minded that I could do something other than study—that I was more than just a mind—so I asked him to teach me to run. I had never run before, unless there was a free pumpkin spice anything to run toward. Or an Ann Taylor Loft sale. Or it was double stamp day at my favorite coffee shop. You get the idea. And so it came as a huge surprise to me when he told me I was actually a good run-ner. After our first long run together, Dad commented: *"You don't seem tired at all. You have an endurance that I think you don't even know that you have."* It remains one of the best compliments of my life. With the name John, I am reminded that I have inherited my father's discipline and resilience. Being named for someone else ties you inextricably to that person, for better or for worse. There are days when I wear my glasses instead of my contacts, look in the mirror and think: *"Oh, God. Add two inches and a mustache, and I am my father."*

My father had big dreams for me. After it was clear that I would pursue higher education, his dream was for me to become president of Samford University, my beloved alma mater (*I'm not waiting by the phone for that*). But that was never my dream. Nor was it my dream to be defined solely by what I did for a living or by my identity as "Dr. Forlini." It's a name I've worked hard to achieve, but it is equal parts blessing and curse. It is a blessing because it is something conferred, an honor bestowed on me not because of any particular intelligence, but as a testament to the resilience inherited from my father. It is also a name that only my students call me, a reminder of the traditions of the academy in which I have made my vocational home.

Still, the name "Dr. Forlini" carries with it a kind of weight, a burden of being seen as a scholar instead of a person. The burden of unwelcome distance on the part of students who have come to reverence authority, or of fellow churchgoers who will not simply let me be "Noel" in a Sunday school class. Over time, answering to the name "Dr. Forlini" represented an exhausting, internal tug of war that I increasingly felt around my vocational identity. Somewhere around the third year of my wilderness in Waco, I wasn't at all sure who I wanted to be.

"*Noel, I can sense how tired you are, how isolated you feel in this season.*" The words of my spiritual director were simple, and she spoke them softly. Still, somewhere deep inside, I breathed a sigh of relief: someone, finally, *saw me*. With a grace quiet and exposing, she said my name and pulled back the curtain on all that I had been hiding. In her words, I sensed an invitation from God to speak about my life. And so it all came pouring out, tears on a dry ground, this spilled truth of my life: "*I feel so awfully alone. The people who love me, the people who know me for more than what I do for a living, are all far away from here. I can't see them. I can't touch them. And I have no way to articulate how this all feels over the phone, when they have to care for crying babies and do their own work. I don't know how to say this in a sound bite. I don't know how to say it at all. All I know is that I can't see God, I can't hear God, and I feel completely abandoned. I feel so profoundly lonely.*"

It was a loneliness that had turned into a clinical depression, one that hampered my ability to keep running, to keep persevering, in that season. My depression was compounded by the fact that for years even prior to this particular wilderness experience,

I had also felt an acute isolation from another source of comfort—the Bible. It was something that I didn't share with a lot of people, and it was something that marked a real change from my younger self. When I was just a young seminary student, one of my classmates remarked, *"You really love the Bible. There are definitely easier electives you could be taking other than 'Exposition of the Minor Prophets' and 'Exegesis of Romans'!"* I hadn't thought about it until someone else pointed it out to me: my transcript during seminary listed just about every Bible course Beeson Divinity School offered.

I had come to love the Bible for the first time when, as a twenty-three-year-old first-time Sunday school teacher, I also came to love the thirteen-year-old girls I was teaching. I saw that the Bible could speak to their hearts, and to their hurts. It was this experience that drew me to seminary in the first place. Seminary shaped me into a person who saw the Bible as a source of spiritual formation and healing.

By the time I had graduated with my doctorate, however, I had been shaped into a different kind of person—a biblical scholar. It was a transformation that, for a long time, left me in a quandary about what to do with my faith.

I'm not quite sure how it happened, but the innocent twenty-three-year-old who had taught the Bible with such joy was now a person who delivered academic papers about the Bible to an elite group of intellectuals. In the ballrooms of expensive hotels multiple times each year, a handful of scholars debate the meaning of an obscure Hebrew word with enough gusto to suggest that their very lives depended on it. While we pat ourselves on the back for laying aside our yearning for God, as though it was a shameful childhood phase we ought to outgrow, the folks in the pews go hungry for the Word of God. I had become a scholar, and without realizing it, a real ass.

One thing that some scholars share, to our detriment, is reading with feigned, smug detachment. Making a pretense of scholarly objectivity, as if such a thing were possible, many of us are observers rather than participants. *"What does the text say?"* is often a bulwark protecting us from actual feeling, actual engagement, with our own lives and with the lives of God's people. But God's story always pulls us into its pages, inviting us not to observe—but to participate. Slowly, I began to sense God's invitation of grace to befriend several biblical characters as if for the first time. As I turned page after page in the biblical story, I suddenly found myself not in the posture of a scholar, but of a fellow traveler. God extended an invitation to take my place alongside biblical characters who felt abandoned in the wilderness. I'm not quite sure *how* it happened, *but* it happened.

Either way, it was God's grace to me, and it came out of nowhere, as grace often does.

It must have come out of nowhere for Hagar too, that slave girl who encountered God at a spring of water in the middle of the wilderness (Gen 16; 21:8–21). An Egyptian in a land not her own, Hagar's whole life had been a wilderness. Throughout her story, Abraham and Sarah never refer to her by name. Instead, when she is referred to at all, they refer to her merely as "slave girl." Their treatment of her is classically dehumanizing: she is a slave, a thing to be used and discarded. She does not speak, nor is she spoken to. Utterly voiceless, Hagar is forced to bear a child for the barren Sarah, the one too busy laughing to trust in the promises of God. In the end, Sarah regrets the whole thing, and Hagar and her child are discarded, forced to flee to the wilderness. A victim of abuse, did she have enough resilience to hope for a different life? Forced to bear a child for someone else, how did she feel about that child? Did she love him? Did she want him? Through it all, we are not told how she actually feels. Of course, nobody asks her anyway, because throughout her story, no one actually sees *her*: her fears, her isolation, or the fact that she's so tired that wilderness actually seems like a good place to rest.

It must have come as the shock of her life when God found her in the middle of the wilderness. It's not just that God finds her literally, although he does. No, God *finds her*—finds her in the way that we, all of us, long to be found. He finds her in the way that Jesus described in language both quotidian and haunting—like a woman sweeping a house to find just one coin; like a man going after the one sheep that ran off; and like an overly effusive father running from the front porch to welcome home his prodigal son. It's in this same way that Hagar is found. She is the something precious that has been lost. And so are we, all of us, that precious treasure that gets lost, runs away, that God goes on looking for and finding all our lives. God finds us all because, well, God always finds what he's looking for.

When God finds Hagar, for the first time someone actually calls her by her name—"Hagar, slave of Sarah, where have you come from and where are you going?" (Gen 16:8 NRSV). I imagine that hearing her name—probably for the first time in a long while—jolted her awake, reminded her that she had a story beyond the one written for her by Abraham and Sarah. Hagar, the one whose name means something like "the Stranger," or "the Wanderer," or "the Resident Alien," is addressed by God.

Of course it's not that God doesn't know where she's been and where she's going. While she probably felt misplaced, God doesn't need GPS coordinates to find her—God has seen her all along. She hasn't been misplaced. No, God's question isn't one about location—it's a question that invites her to tell her story—something akin to asking her where it hurts. Of course it's not because God doesn't know where she hurts. While she probably feels unheard, God doesn't need to hear Hagar's story—he has known her story before the first page was ever written. What she needs is to feel seen, to feel heard, and to tell her story herself. And that's exactly what she does. It all comes pouring out, tears on a dry ground, this spilled truth of her life: *"I'm running away from this terrible home and from these terrible people, and I'm in this terrible wilderness, waiting to die."*

God listens to Hagar's affliction and responds with another name—*Ishmael*, the name God gives to the child she will bear. *Ishmael*, which means "God hears" (Gen 16:11). On that terrible day next to a well of water in the wilderness, God tells Hagar that he has seen her, he has heard her, and he is birthing something new inside her. In naming Ishmael, God names a new life for Hagar, a

63

new identity, and a newly unfolding relationship with himself. It must have come as the surprise of her life—that in the middle of the wilderness, God would offer to Hagar new life.

It came as the surprise of my life, too. It was summer, and I had made the long drive from Waco to Sumatanga. When I had been there in February during one of the lowest points of my life, I had poured out my heart to God, ending my prayer with these words: *"I need grace, and I need it in abundance. I cannot save myself in this season, or in any other. Noel has been defeated. I am yours. I need a new name. I don't want to be Noel anymore. I want the name you give me. I want to be whoever you want me to be. I don't know who this new person will be but I do know to whom she will belong."* At the time, even I did not understand exactly what I meant by those words, and why my name found its way into my prayer. When I arrived at Sumatanga again that summer, the experience was, as always, like drinking water from a deep well. One moment, however, was a particularly graced surprise.

I can't explain the feeling in the room that day, other than to say that God felt present. There we were, about sixty of us, crowded together in a small room, where we were asked to hold hands and pray. I was seated next to Sandy, whose friendship has become one of the greatest blessings to emerge out of monk camp. When the prayer ended, she continued to hold my hand, her blue eyes piercing into mine: *"It's funny, every time I look at you, at your face, I know your name is Noel, but I just think: Hope. Your name is Hope. It's so strange."*

I'm not sure *how* it happened, *but* it happened.

Either way, it was God's grace to me, and it came out of nowhere, as grace often does.

I know of no other way to describe it than that it felt like a baptism, like water from a deep well.

And here we arrive again at Hagar's well, *Beer-lahai-roi*, "The Well of the Living One Who Sees Me." Hagar, the only woman in all the Bible both to name God and her experience of God. To God, she gives the name El-Roi, which means, "the God who sees me." And she memorializes the experience by naming the well

64

Beer-lahai-roi, "the Well of the Living One Who Sees Me." Suddenly, an ordinary well and an ordinary spot at the edge of the wilderness becomes sacred space. And an otherwise terrible day becomes a day when God offers a word of hope. It is a reminder to us all that God hasn't misplaced us—God sees us, God hears us, and God offers a promise of new life in the midst of our pain. God sees us—and in spite of all the other names we might go by, God names what he sees in us.

God used Sandy to name what he saw in me that day—*Hope*. Sandy could have never known the power of the truth she had named that day, or that God had been whispering the word *Hope* over me for a long time.

Hope—the first word I saw written on a table in my little room at Camp Sumatanga. *Hope*—a theme I had been asked to preach on just a few months prior. *Hope*—a word I heard sung as I settled myself quietly in my friend's living room, while she finished giving a voice lesson: *"Hope in the Lord, and he will give you the desires of your heart . . ."* her student sang. *Hope*—my hopes to come home to Alabama, to come home to being shaped by the Bible once again, to come home to God, to come home to myself. *Hope*—the strong feeling that I was a heart person trapped in a head profession and my fervent desire for that to change. *Hope*—the name my mother nearly called me. God used Sandy that day to name me *Hope*. I'm not sure *how* it happened, *but* it happened.

Either way, it was God's grace to me, and it came out of nowhere, as grace often does.

Throughout the Bible, hope is linked to something we are *waiting for*, and to two related realities: *pain* and *change*.

Famously, Paul put it this way: "For in hope we were saved. Now hope that is seen is not hope. For who hopes for what is seen? But if we hope for what we do not see, we wait for it with patience" (Rom 8:24–25 NRSV). For Paul, hope is tied to some unseen, future work of God, the consummation of all that is into the love of Christ. Until that unseen moment, we wait as exiles in a land not our own, with the writer of Hebrews agreeing with Paul: "Now faith is the assurance of things hoped for, the conviction of things not seen" (Heb 11:1 NRSV).

To be people of hope is to be people who wait for the consummation of all that is into the love of Christ. We wait for God to enfold all that is—all that is in the larger wilderness of this world—and all that is in the smaller wildernesses in which we find ourselves—into the love of Christ. To be people of hope is to be people who wait—*with God*, in wilderness. And this waiting is not without pain, as Paul acknowledges.

Hope is a posture that involves waiting, groaning, travailing, like Hagar in labor with her child (Rom 8:22–23). Hope waits for new life to unfold, for something new to be born—even for a new name or a new identity. Indeed, the writers of the Old Testament understand *Qavah*, the verb for "Hope," and *Tikvah*, the noun for "Hope," as something that twines, that is bound together, like a cord. It is something that we wait for, something that we can hold onto, like a promise. To the Israelites in exile, Isaiah offers this reassuring word: "But those who wait for the LORD shall renew their strength, they shall mount up with wings like eagles, they shall run and not be weary, they shall walk and not faint" (Isa 40:31 NRSV). Isaiah understood *hope* as that which bound God's covenant people together, transforming both their circumstances and their hearts. Likewise, the psalmist advised the waiting, exiled community: "Be still before the LORD, and wait patiently for him" (Ps 37:7 NRSV). Using the related word *Chul*, the psalmist's advice to "wait patiently" is also linked to pain—and change. *Chul*, to "wait patiently," describes a kind of twisting, especially to twist and writhe as in childbirth. To be a person of hope, then, is to wait through the pain of new life being born.

In Hagar's life, all that waiting, all that hope, had in fact created an entwined cord—a birth cord connecting her body to the life of Ishmael, her son. Ishmael is the very embodiment of Hagar's hope. Ishmael is the something new that is born, a child who would embody Hagar's new understanding that God had seen her and heard her. In naming Ishmael, God names a new life for Hagar, a new identity, and a newly unfolding relationship with himself. It must have come as the surprise of her life—that in the middle of the wilderness, God would offer to Hagar new life.

Either way, it was God's grace to her, and it came out of nowhere, as grace often does.

Through Sandy's words, grace came out of nowhere for me, too. She could not have known that I had spent most of my adult life hoping with God for things that seemed impossible, a kind of unhealed, Pauline wound in my side (2 Cor 12:7–10). Find your wound, and I'm convinced you'll find the truth about your life. And the truth of my life in that season was that I, like Hagar, had felt abandoned, too tired to run anymore, and too tired to hope any longer.

To Sandy, all I could manage to say was *"Thank you,"* as I wiped a few tears from my eyes and excused myself from the room. And once again, there it was, water from a deep well, tears on a dry ground, this spilled out the truth of my life. I know of no other way to describe it than that it felt like a baptism.

Beer-lahai-roi, "the Well of the Living God Who Sees Me."

Hagar, one who names the well, is incredulous: "Have I really seen God and remained alive after seeing him?" (Gen 16:13 NRSV)

And her incredulousness makes perfect sense—the larger injunction of the Old Testament was that no one could see God and live (Exod 33:20). Yet Hagar, this strange woman in this strange land, catches a glimpse of this hope(full) God *and is not named by him but names him.*

There's something about being in wilderness and being met by God there that textures our relationship with him; we can name him because we've experienced him in a personal, affective way. It changes us, and so we can name what that time with him has been, because we've seen him in a real way. Still, in asking Hagar the question—"Where have you come from and where are you going?" (Gen 16:13)—God acknowledges that while it is she who claims to have "seen" him, *he has really seen her.* And what he must have seen in her that day was a woman desperately in need of hope.

Hagar, the one whose name means "the Stranger," gives birth to Ishmael, whose name means "God hears." And she names the experience—*Beer-lahai-roi*, "the Well of the Living God Who Sees Me."

That day at Camp Sumatanga, God also named a new life for me, a new identity, and a newly unfolding relationship with himself. It came as the surprise of my life—that in the middle of my wilderness season, this hope(full) God would offer me life.

I'm not sure *how* it happened, *but* it happened.

Either way, it came out of nowhere, as grace often does.

7

Building Houses

I NEVER WANTED TO purchase a house in Texas. Rationally, I knew that buying a house didn't commit us to Texas forever—houses are bought and sold every day. Still, something about it felt permanent, so we put it off as long as we could. While the Israelites lived in tents in the wilderness, we chose an apartment, the modern person's option for picking up their stakes and moving at a moment's notice.

Three summers later, I sat on the back patio of a friend's house in Alabama, where I shared my angst about wanting to move home. Her heartache on my behalf was palpable, and with a sigh of resignation almost too deep for words, she said, *"I guess you just do what the prophet Jeremiah told the Israelites to do in exile—build houses and plant a garden until the Lord moves you home."*

Later that summer, we purchased a house in Texas. It was a cute house, a wonderful starter home, with one irritating feature— the builder chose a front door with a Texas star in the glass. I'm sure he assumed a Texan would buy the house and love that little attention to detail. As an Alabamian living in a Texan exile, the first thing I did was to cover up that Texas star in the window with an Alabama football wreath. The truth is, I don't understand or even watch football, what most Alabamians consider a moral failing. I just wanted something that reminded me of home to cover up that terrible Texas star.

There are lots of ways you can build a house without really living in it. Usually, you unpack the necessary things—clothes, of course, and all of the kitchen essentials—in my case, the coffee pot. Then there's your favorite lamp to read by, maybe an end table or two, but the walls might be bare for a long time, and many other things might stay in boxes in the garage. In the beginning, you unpack just enough to get you by.

I'll leave the extra dishes in boxes in the garage, we'll never invite people over anyway, you reason.

Holiday decorations? Why would I unpack those? We won't be spending Christmas here.

All my books? No, I have too many—I'll just unpack the ones I really need.

You can buy a house but never really make it a home. Lots of things can stay in boxes so that you can move away as soon as the opportunity presents itself. You can leave the yard empty, never planting anything. Introverts like me find it easy never to meet the neighbors. If you stay aloof enough, you never draw close enough to anyone to invite them over, anyway. You can keep the blinds closed, the doors locked, and spend all your time indoors. You can build a house without ever really making it a home. It's there, but it's a place of self-protection rather than a place in which to invite other people. If you're diligent enough, you can build a beautiful house in which to hide yourself, and you can cover it with a nice Alabama wreath that keeps all the Texans away. The heart, I've discovered, is a lot like that.

Theologians call it the false self, and it's the house you build to protect your heart. Ultimately, the false self is a house built on fear. Fear of not being enough. Fear of having to earn the love of other people. Fear of having to earn the love of God. Fear that you cannot be loved or even liked exactly as you are. Of course, our very adult, pious self may stand up tall, shoulders high, announcing our worth like a clanging cymbal. We are educated. We have made our way in the world. We are good parents. We are good people. We are Sunday school teachers, deacons, the first people the pastor calls on to teach or preach in his absence. We can take pride in all those things, never consciously aware that these very childlike questions linger under the surface: *"Do you like me? Am I okay? Do you find me acceptable?"*[1] We may never voice these questions aloud, but whenever we exaggerate who we are, or lay it on with our gifts in the hopes that people will notice us, respect us, and love us, we can be sure that the false self is at work.[2]

Facebook culture highlights the false self (or the false face) in a deceptively simple way. Facebook gives us a platform to count how many "likes" we have, now even how many "loves" we have. We can post our pictures (*only the best ones, of course*), we can post our ideas (*only the edited ones, of course*), and obsessively check the number of "likes" we have, even collecting "friends" in a staggering number. Who are my "followers," and what level of wit, intellectual sophistication, or spiritual wisdom must I display to make sure they keep "following" me? Do you like me? Do you like my ideas? We can become like a child clamoring for attention and love, even as we are uncertain we are worthy of it, the very definition of the false self.

The false self is the person we think we should be but are not. It's the person we want others to think we are, usually the one who is able to love perfectly, who is wise and all-knowing, and who is in control of her life. The false self thrives on success and achievement,[3] usually rooting itself in whatever it is we think we lacked in childhood.[4] Rooted in our insecurities and deficiencies, real or perceived, the false self always comes from the broken home of the heart. This may have little to do with what kind of home we actually grew up in. Even the warmest and most life-giving of childhood houses is still built in the neighborhood of this world, a place where sin and suffering touch our hearts at an early age. Our hearts are broken because we live in a broken, fragmented world, and the whole of life is giving ourselves over to the God

1. Haase, *Coming Home to Your True Self*, 44.
2. Fryling, *Mirror for the Soul*, 23–35.
3. Fryling, *Mirror for the Soul*, 25.
4. Haase, *Coming Home to Your True Self*, 47.

who can heal and integrate our hearts once more. And so the false self comes from the broken home of fear.

I must have been about nine years old when the picture was taken. Wearing a flowered dress and a big white bow, I stood dutifully in front of the family hearth. In my hands, an academic award, the first of many I would work for and earn. In the picture, I'm not really smiling—more the look of tired resignation from a nine-year-old who probably didn't want her picture taken. From a very young age, I learned to earn love and status through academic achievement. It's no wonder, then, that little Noel grew up to become "Dr. Forlini." Did I pursue graduate education because I felt called to it? Yes, of that I'm certain. Did I also pursue graduate education because academic achievement was the house on which my false self was built? Yes, of that I'm also certain.

This isn't altogether bad. In my case, God used my drive for achievement to help me pursue what he was calling me to in a particular season of my life. God can also use the false self to perform a protective work. Just as not every person is a safe person to enter our actual homes, not every person is safe enough to enter the home of our heart. The false self can create a necessary distance, a locked door with an Alabama football wreath on it. Not every person is safe enough to know who we truly are. But there comes a time when the false self no longer serves, and when that time comes, God usually makes his way to our house.

Interestingly, it wasn't any of the houses where I lived in Alabama that God came to, knocking on the door to tell me about my false self. No, it was that house I built in the wilderness of exile, the one with the Texas star in the glass on the front door. God made his way to that house, the one I built in the wilderness of exile. And I imagine that when he arrived at my door, he chuckled at my wreath, because, God knows, I know nothing about football. And all of this is grace—both his laughter and the fact that he came to my house at all.

And the conversation goes something like this:

"You know this isn't really going to keep all the Texans out, right?"

And just for fun, he adds: *"Noel, who plays quarterback for Alabama?"*

"What's a quarterback?" I respond.

"Just what I thought," he laughs. *"Now open the door."*

Maybe I'm a slow learner, but it's taken me a long time to realize that whenever God enters the house of my heart, he's not just stopping by to drop off a casserole. Whenever I choose to open the door of my heart to God, my house isn't my own anymore. My house—my heart—belongs to God. He can come in, and if he wants, just sit and talk about the remains of the day over a cup of coffee (*God takes his coffee with cream and sugar, in case you were wondering*). We can laugh together, enjoy one another's company, and it can be a pleasant visit. Or God can enter my living room and tell me that my furniture is old and needs to be replaced (*since I've had most of my furniture since college, I'd say that's fair*).

"This looked good a long time ago, but it doesn't really suit you anymore," he might say.

Or, *"I don't know why you bought this in the first place. This looks like someone else's style, not yours. You do you, girl"* (*God calls me "girl" in my imagination*).

If I'm having a particularly stubborn day, I might bristle at God's projected remodeling. New furniture might cost me more than I'm willing to pay, or I might want to keep hanging on to the old stuff, because it's served me well since I was eighteen, so why shouldn't I keep it? And on and on it goes, these futile negotiations with God. Letting God into my heart and then not letting him have his way is fickle behavior, and it's foolish. God created my heart, God dwells inside my heart. Like my house, it's his to renovate.

If we let him, that's what God does in the wilderness—he renovates our heart.

The wilderness is the Way Home, God whispers.

The Way Home to God, the Way Home to your true self.

The wilderness is the Way Home.

Yet it is not without pain—this renovation of the heart that takes place in the wilderness. The pain doesn't come when the Rooms To Go truck delivers that shiny new sofa. No, that's a good day, an exciting day, one often rooted in gratitude. The pain comes in the removal of the old, and in the waiting for the new to be delivered to your house. The pain comes in parting with the old furniture—the kind with holes in the pillow cushions, rips in the fabric, stains on the coffee table—we've been trying to hide them or to patch them for far too long. It's time to throw them out completely, and it's time to do the costly work of replacing those things with something new.

The pain also comes while we wait for the Rooms To Go truck to arrive. The trouble is, sometimes we wait in an empty house for longer than we'd like. We've removed that beat-up old chair, the one with the dog hair on every square inch of fabric. The trouble is, once it's gone, we don't always know immediately what goes in its place. So we examine the living room, knowing we'll need another chair, but not sure what kind of fabric would work, or what color scheme would match the walls. And so we wait. The heart waits, too. But God doesn't play games with us. The prophet Jeremiah makes it clear: "When you come looking for me, you'll find me. Yes, when you get serious about finding me and want it more than anything else, I'll make sure you won't be disappointed" (Jer 29:12 *The Message*).

Pulling up, taking apart, tearing down—and waiting on the new arrival, starting over, building and planting—that's at the heart of God's house renovation in the wilderness. And that's the part that's painful.

Even so, *the wilderness is the Way Home*, God whispers.
The Way Home to God, the Way Home to your true self.
The wilderness is the Way Home.

Homes, doors—these are familiar images in our own, ordinary lives. They are also familiar images in the lives of the exiled children of Israel, used to great effect by the prophet Jeremiah. Referred to throughout church history as the "weeping prophet," Jeremiah produced, by nearly all accounts, some of the most melancholy literature we have in all the Bible. All his weeping, and the weeping of the people in exile, makes perfect sense. This is literature of suffering and surrender, and it is the literature of our lives, too. Pulling up and starting over—this was the hard word Jeremiah was asked to deliver in a hard place. He was told to advise the Israelites to build houses, plant gardens, and prepare to stay awhile in the wilderness of exile from their home (Jer 29:4–7).

There is a necessary surrender to all of this. When we realize that, for however long (*perhaps for always?*), God's plan for us is different from our plan for ourselves, inevitably, we find ourselves in the crucible of the wilderness. We must allow the wilderness to do its purifying—or crucifying—work.

Am I willing to submit my will, my whole will, my whole self, to this God who has entered into the house of my heart, seeking to renovate it?

Do I want God more than anything else?

If God never gives me the thing I want most in the world, will I still love him?

Do I trust God in every season? If the house renovation takes place in a winter of grief, will I trust God? If the house renovation takes place during a summer of joy, will I trust God?

These are the questions the wilderness puts to us, and these are the very questions of our lives.

There is only one answer, either yes or no. The answer is never "*Yes, but . . .*" or, "*Yes, and . . .*"

The answer is either yes or no.

And if the answer is "no," there must be a house renovation.

So we are told to build houses in the wilderness, and when God comes knocking on our door and we agree to let him in, we must expect him to have a good look around, to assess what fits and what doesn't.

When God entered the houses that the Israelites had built for themselves in the wilderness of exile, God found them to be fickle, trusting him sometimes and not at other times, exercising their own will sometimes, bending to his will at other times. Toward the end of God's visit to the Israelites' houses, they themselves exclaim: "You trained me well. You broke me, a wild yearling horse, to the saddle. Now put me, trained and obedient, to use. You are my God. After those years of running loose, I repented" (Jer 31:18–19 *The*

Message). What God requires here is not sadomasochism, not un-
healthy shame. No, what God requires is a right understanding of
who is in control.

Plain and simple, nothing mysterious about it—obedience
must be learned. There is a hopefulness to all of this, of course,
but it's a hopefulness rooted in suffering. And we often learn obedience through suffering. Scandalously, even Jesus learned obedience through suffering: "Although he was a Son," the writer of
Hebrews says (Heb 5:8). Suffering doesn't magically transform us
into God's children—we are already God's children. What it does is
ready us for use, not through divine sadism but through maturing
us, rooting us more deeply in the love of God, so that we might be
a blessing to others. *"It is doubtful,"* A. W. Tozer wrote, *"that God
can bless a man greatly until He has hurt him deeply."*[5] We become
a vessel for God's healing in the lives of others not by escaping our
woundedness, but by living through it. We are to become, as Henri
Nouwen wrote, wounded healers.[6] And so we must give up the old
ways.

The wilderness is the place where we are to lay the old ways
down, to make space for the new thing that God is doing.

Give me room to work, I heard God whisper.

The wilderness is the Way Home.

The Way Home to God, the Way Home to your true self.

The wilderness is the Way Home.

So we have to carve out a little room in which God can work.
We have to make space for God.

In laying our old ways down, we make space for God to work.
We clear out a little room.

In my own house, I'm starting in the room where I've kept my
hope. For as long as I can remember, I've kept my hope duct-taped
inside a box labeled "Achievement." My false self packed that up
nice and tight, nearly impossible to get open. That little nine-year-
old in the flowered dress holding that academic award grew up and
put quite a few awards in that box. Over time, all my hopes were

5. Tozer, *Root of the Righteous*, 165.

6. Nouwen, *Wounded Healer*.

put there—that if I just worked hard enough, had enough letters behind my name, enough certifications on my resume, ran enough races, chose to do all the hard things I could think to do, then I would find my way home. Home to God, home to myself, home, finally, to Alabama. The trouble with that is, in spite of my best efforts, I'm still in Texas, and I'm still that girl with the flowered dress holding the box labeled "Achievement." I have to let that box go, clear out the room in which I've kept it.

There's nothing particularly wrong with achievement.

The only trouble is, it isn't grace.

The only trouble is, it's not the right place in which to put my hope.

In the end, placing my hope in my achievement doesn't just exclude God's grace—it also excludes the present moment, what God *is doing*, right now, here, in this present moment. Surrender to the life that is your own—it's the only one that you have. God may be everywhere, but he is also only in this present moment— the "now" of your life. "Now" is the only place where you can be transformed. God is doing something new, and he's doing it "now." So lay the old ways down, lay the old life down, and put hope in the right box. God is doing something new in the crucible of this present moment.

I am making a Way in the wilderness, God says (Isa 43:19; Isa 40:3).

The wilderness is the Way Home.

The Way Home to God, the Way Home to your true self.

The wilderness is the Way Home.

The only place God is—is now.[7]

God is in the wilderness. And that's the place where hope is to be found. So what do I do, while I wait for God to bring those hopes into full bloom? Maybe I plant a few seeds. If the new thing, if resurrection, hasn't happened just yet, maybe we practice it, as Wendell Berry said.[8] I've always wanted an herb garden, so I think I'll start there.

7. Mills, Upper Room Academy for Spiritual Formation Lecture.

8. Berry, *"Manifesto: The Mad Farmer Liberation Front."*

Wilderness is the place where we learn where to put our hope. Our hope belongs not in a box marked "Achievement," sealed too tight to open. No, our hope belongs in whatever room God happens to be in, in an open box labeled, "What God *Is Doing*."

That's at the heart of what Jeremiah says to the Israelites in the wilderness of their own exile from home. It's a word we give to people on the cusp of a new thing, all the time. It's a word I've given—with great hope—to my students who graduate and move on to whatever new thing God is doing in their lives. It's the word we know best from Jeremiah, if we know any of his words at all, and it's this one: "I know what I'm doing. I have it all planned out—plans to take care of you, not abandon you, plans to give you the future you hope for" (Jer 29:11 *The Message*).

The only future worth hoping for is the future God has planned. So in the wilderness, carve out a little space, clear out a room, and wait for God in the wilderness.

The wilderness is the Way Home.

The Way Home to God, the Way Home to your true self.

The wilderness is the Way Home.

8

Coming Home

It's about a ten-mile drive off the interstate, winding your way through country roads, on the way to Sumatanga. You're surrounded (*hugged, really*) on all sides by trees dotting those rolling hills I love so much—the ones that seem to reach clear up to the Alabama skyline.

The first time I arrived there, my pastor, Gary, picked me up from the airport and drove me and a few new friends to the camp. He's a monk camp graduate himself, so it was special for both of us.

As we pulled off the interstate and started down those same country roads I would drive for the next two years, Gary grinned and mused aloud, to no one in particular: *"You know, I bet a place where you're surrounded for extended periods of time by other people would be hard for someone who's an introvert."*

He knows me well.

"Maybe," I said. *"But I bet a place where you're asked to keep silence for extended periods of time would be hard for someone who's always talking."*

He grinned. I know him well, too.

Everyone else in the car was oblivious.

Just as we exchanged our good-natured jibes, the trees seemed to part, and I saw it for the first time, the sign that read: *"Camp Sumatanga: Welcome Home."*

It was the strangest thing—for the first time in two years, I felt like I could breathe.

Whenever you arrive at Sumatanga, you check in first at the front desk, where you get instructions about the schedule and your room key. I would later learn the room key was a formality—no one actually uses it at Sumatanga. In the back of the lobby, I saw what would become a familiar place for me, the little fireplace and the cozy chairs, and stenciled on the floor in front of the fireplace, what I discovered was the meaning of *Sumatanga*: "A place of rest and vision."

I was given directions to my lodging—Building Five, which is where they put the young folks because it's a bit of a hike.

Room 508, the room with my name on the door—the same room that would be mine, every three months, for the next two years.

When I walked into my room, the first thing that hit me was not how quaint those quarters were (*which they were*) but instead the words I heard so loudly within myself that I was almost knocked over: *"Welcome Home."*

I can count on one hand the number of times I have "heard" God actually speak to me in that way. Those words were striking, both for their brevity and because I knew, somewhere deep down inside myself, that these were the truest words I'd ever hear—*Welcome Home.*

It was the strangest thing—for the first time in two years, I felt like I could breathe.

While it is true that Sumatanga just happens to be located in Alabama, the place I call home, I believe God was welcoming me home in a deeper sense. That day, I stepped over a threshold—an entry, a point of beginning, a new way of envisioning my life. While I had built a house for my false self, founded on fear and achievement and covered up with an Alabama wreath, God had built a home for me, a place where I could truly live. When I stepped over the threshold that day, the disparate parts of myself began not just to touch—they began to embrace. In bringing all the disparate parts of myself together, God was welcoming me home—home to my true self. As the old hymn puts it, "No more a stranger nor a guest, but like a child at Home."[1]

The truth of the matter is that we can build all the houses we want, but only Jesus makes a house a home. Throughout the Gospels, Jesus tells those thick-headed friends of his—the ones bumbling about, focusing on the wrong things—*how much these friends remind me of myself, of all my own friends, and of every person that I know*—you've got to lose yourselves to find yourselves (Mark 8:35). While many different theologians have written about and developed the concept of the true self, the idea begins with Jesus.

Later, Jesus would tell those same thickheaded, bumbling friends: *Trust me, I'm going home to prepare a home for you. My Father has all the space in the world in his home, and he's got just the right place for you. The room is ready, whenever you are* (John 14:1–7).

The true self makes its home in the love of God.

While Jesus is the first to talk about the true self, and Paul would certainly build on it using different imagery (Eph 4:22–24; 2 Cor 3:18), I first *truly heard* the idea at Sumatanga, through the writings of Thomas Merton.

"To be a saint is to be myself," Merton wrote.[2]

This doesn't mean we're sinless—far from it. It means we can live spontaneously, in the here and now of the present moment, like a child, dependent and in relationship with others and with God, that most important of Other(s).[3] The true self is that little child, the one Jesus bids to come unto himself, the one without inhibition, without guile, totally honest before God, totally honest before herself, moving through the world sincerely and in God's Spirit. The true self is that little child who is confident in the love that God has for him, able to embrace and to be embraced. Ultimately, self-acceptance is the hallmark of the true self,[4] not in a

1. "My Shepherd Will Supply My Need."
2. Merton, *New Seeds of Contemplation*, 31.
3. Haase, *Coming Home To Your True Self*, 18.
4. Fryling, *Mirror for the Soul*, 33.

New Age, Oprah Winfrey, positive self-talk kind of way (*I've got nothing at all against Oprah, by the way, and I'll be glad to appear on her show if Kelly Clarkson doesn't want to book me*). No, this is a radical self-acceptance that settles so deeply into your bones that you can hear God's abiding *"yes"* over your life.

The true self is the person God envisioned me to be, before my parents ever met one another and instilled a little bit of nature, a little bit of nurture, and brought me into the world. The true self is the child God made, before I ever thought I had to earn my way home. The true self is the child God made, before I learned to listen to other voices, the ones that said, *"You want to be taken seriously? Teach students to think critically. Leave the heart stuff to pastors, people in churches. Produce scholarship, make a name for yourself—hide your heart."* The true self is the child God made, before I ever learned to be afraid—afraid of the world, afraid of living from my heart, afraid of living authentically—afraid.

No more a stranger nor a guest, but like a child at Home.

To be the child God made, with all my gifts and graces, love of words, love of fireplaces and easy chairs, warm coffee and good mystery novels. To be a writer. To be a teacher who seeks, above all else, to educate the *heart* of my students. To be a teacher who sits with students, with an open heart and an open Bible, trusting in the slow work of God to shape their lives. To be a spiritual director and a wife and a friend.

No more a stranger nor a guest, but like a child at Home.
The true self makes its home in the love of God.

Whenever you come home, there it is—that familiar Voice, the one who has been lullabying over you your whole life. You can call it the Voice of God, you can call it the Sound of the Genuine, you can call it your coffee finally kicking in—you can call it anything you like. Whatever you call it, there it is—lullabying softly like a bird nestled in the trees in the dark, announcing the morning. Lullabying softly, like the sound of coffee brewing, announcing the time for morning prayer. Lullabying softly, like the Sound of the Genuine, that which is most true and sacred about the human heart. This Voice lullabies in wilderness spaces where all seems lost. At the end of self, you find its beginning. To come to the end of yourself, to die to yourself, is to be on the brink of everything else. In the wilderness, dying to yourself is God's severest grace—because at the edge of the wilderness, a darkened pathway of grace leads you home. A Voice lullabying in the wilderness, *"Welcome Home."*

When I finally heard that Voice, I stood inside the threshold of my little room at Sumatanga, a jumble of broken pieces and a jumble of broken selves, and heard an invitation to pick up the shards of my broken life, to hold them up to the light, and to make them into something beautiful. It's a Voice, I suspect, that sings the same lullaby over us all—*pick up the shards of your broken life, and hold them up to the light. What beautiful thing will you make from them?*

After all this time, I know one thing for certain—God doesn't waste any of it.

The true self makes its home in the love of God.
No more a stranger nor a guest, but like a child at Home.
Your room is ready, whenever you are.

There's something poignant about being *"Welcomed Home"* to a place where you will keep returning. Much like my return to Sumatanga every three months, coming home is a process, and we'll never fully arrive in this life. For me, it was a reminder that, in Henri Nouwen's words, we have to keep coming home to God.[5] Life with God is like that—we keep coming home all our lives. We keep returning to God. Having lived all my life with myself, I know that I'm the thickheaded one, the one who's always bumbling about, forgetful that God has already created a home for me. And so I keep on coming home all my life. I will keep on coming home until the day I die. In the meantime, I just do my best, however falteringly, to trust the slow work of God. I trust that the One who began a good work in me, as Paul said, will carry it to completion. We keep on coming home all our lives, because home is still something that we're searching for. Ultimately, we were made for a

5. Nouwen, *Inner Voice of Love.* Journeying home is a persistent theme throughout Nouwen's writings.

home that we cannot now see. I may never get to live in Alabama again, but I can still come home.

This rhythm of coming home is important. When I'm not at Sumatanga, I mark my coming home through the daily ritual of brewing coffee. All my life, I have loved coffee. From the first, wanting-to-be-a-grown-up sip of coffee shop cappuccino (*more froth than coffee*), to the coffee I drank at 5 AM over prayer during my seminary days (*what I affectionately called "Java with Jesus"*), to the coffee I prepare for my students when they come to my office, to the early morning coffee I drink out here in the Texas wilderness, when my husband and the rest of the house is still asleep, and it's just quiet enough to hear the birds hum in the dark, to the countless cups of coffee I have shared with friends—this ritual is about connection, relationship, intimacy, the desire to know as I am known. This coffee-making ritual is prayer, the spilling of water over the grounds, the vapor rising into the air, the *crackle, gurgle, crackle, gurgle* sound as it brews—all part of the ritual of making it—is prayer. All this is connection to the One who has loved me before I was born and who will go on loving me after I die. Holding that warm cup in my hands, turning it around, hearing my wedding ring clink gently against the cup as I wait for the coffee to cool—this is a silent prelude to the Sound of the Genuine in the life that is my own—and all this is prayer.

Whatever it is for each of us, we need rituals of return to God and to the true self he has made us to be. When we engage in rituals of return, we catch glimpses of the home that we were made for but cannot see. We engage in these rituals because we need to keep on coming home all our lives—and not just for ourselves. There are people who will stand at our threshold, looking for home. I cannot welcome someone else into a home I have never found. If, however, I have turned on a few lamps and put on the coffee pot, I might be able to make a little room and say to somebody else, *"Sit in that comfortable chair—it's my favorite. Let's listen together to your life for a while."* When you find yourself truly at home, you are able to welcome others into your home also.

This is important because inside every person we meet is a tiny boy or girl wanting to be loved just for who they are. That little boy or girl is the true self, waiting to be welcomed home, and it's a homesickness we all share. And if we've heard that Voice, even for a moment, we can help others hear it too.

Whenever you come home, there is, indeed, a Voice that welcomes you. You can call it the Voice of God, you can call it the Sound of the Genuine, you can call it your coffee finally kicking in—you can call it whatever you like. The name you give it doesn't matter as much as what it says to you: *"I know the journey has been long. I know how tired you must be. I know you've traveled in wilderness for a lot of it. I've been sitting in my rocking chair the whole time, looking out the window, waiting for you to arrive. No, I didn't fall asleep, not even once. All this time, I've been waiting for this moment—to cup your tired, tiny face in my hands and to tell you, 'You've never looked so much like yourself. Welcome home.'"*

Bibliography

Barrett Browning, Elizabeth. *Aurora Leigh.* Victoria, BC: Mint Editions, 2021.

Berry, Wendell. "Manifesto: The Mad Farmer Liberation Front." In *The Mad Farmer Poems,* 19–21. Berkeley: Counterpoint, 2014.

Buechner, Frederick. "The Magnificent Defeat." In *Secrets in the Dark: A Life in Sermons,* 1–8. New York: HarperOne, 2006.

Carretto, Carlo. *The God Who Comes.* New York: Orbis, 1974.

Dillard, Annie. *Pilgrim at Tinker Creek.* New York: HarperPerennial, 2007.

Fryling, Alice. *Mirror for the Soul: A Christian Guide to the Enneagram.* Downers Grove, IL: InterVarsity, 2017.

Haase, Albert. *Coming Home to Your True Self: Leaving the Emptiness of False Attractions.* Downers Grove, IL: InterVarsity, 2008.

Lamott, Anne. *Bird by Bird: Some Instructions on Writing and Life.* New York: Anchor, 1995.

———. *Traveling Mercies: Some Thoughts on Faith.* New York: Pantheon, 1999.

Merton, Thomas. *New Seeds of Contemplation.* New York: New Directions, 2007.

———. *Thoughts in Solitude.* New York: Douglas & McIntryre, 1956.

Mills, Dawn. Upper Room Academy for Spiritual Formation Lecture. Gallant, AL, November 2018.

Mulholland, M. Robert, Jr. *Shaped by the Word: The Power of Scripture in Spiritual Formation.* Nashville: Upper Room, 2000.

Nouwen, Henri. *Finding My Way Home: Pathways to Life and the Spirit.* New York: Crossroad, 2004.

———. *Home Tonight: Further Reflections on the Parable of the Prodigal Son.* New York: Doubleday, 2009.

———. *The Inner Voice of Love: A Journey through Anguish to Freedom.* New York: Image, 1999.

———. *The Wounded Healer.* New York: Doubleday, 1979.

O'Connor, Flannery. *The Habit of Being: Letters of Flannery O'Connor.* New York: Farrar, Straus and Giroux, 1988.

Palmer, Parker. *A Hidden Wholeness: The Journey Toward an Undivided Life.* San Francisco: Jossey-Bass, 2009.

———. *Let Your Life Speak: Listening for the Voice of Vocation.* San Francisco: Jossey-Bass, 2000.

Rohr, Richard. *The Divine Dance: The Trinity and Your Transformation*. London: SPCK, 2016.

Thurman, Howard. "The Sound of the Genuine." Spelman College Commencement Speech, 1980.

Tozer, A. W. *The Root of the Righteous*. Camp Hill, PA: Christian, 1955. Reprint, Chicago: Moody, 2015.